National 5 ENGLISH

PORTFOLIO
WRITING SKILLS

Willie McGuire

SCOTTISH
EXAMINATION
MATERIALS

HODDER
GIBSON
AN HACHETTE UK COMPANY

The Publishers would like to thank the following for permission to reproduce copyright material:

Photo credits: pp4, 6, 14, 39, 69, 83, 97 © Alexander Raths – Fotolia.com; **p4** © mocker_bat – Fotolia; **p7** © Roman Milert – Fotolia.com; **p9** © Photofusion / Rex Features; **p10** © berc – Fotolia.com & © Sailorr – Fotolia; **p11** © ArtFamily – Fotolia.com; **p14** © Zoonar GmbH / Alamy; **p15** © jörn buchheim – Fotolia; **p27** © Jeremy Woodhouse / Photodisc / Getty Images; **p34** © Mike Greenslade / Alamy; **p40** © Iakov Kalinin – Fotolia; **p42** © Frank Micelotta / Getty Images; **p45** © Jaimie Duplass – Fotolia; **p58** © Peter Titmuss / Alamy; **p65** © Salvador Dali, Fundació Gala-Salvador Dalí, DACS, 2013. Photo © Corbis; **p66** © Anthony22 (Wikipedia Creative Commons: http://en.wikipedia.org/wiki/File:Entrance_To_Van_Cortlandt_Park_2012.jpg, http://creativecommons.org/licenses/by-sa/3.0/); **p73** © fotofrank – Fotolia; **p78** © Chris Hellyar – Fotolia; **p87** © Peter Dazeley / Photographer's Choice / Getty Images

Acknowledgements: p19 The history of snowboarding, from http:en.wikipedia.org/Snowboarding; **p24** UK Internet usage report, from http://hexus.net/internet/35265-uk-internet-usage-report-16-adults-havent-online; **p27** Visit Hong Kong, from http://www.tes.co.uk/teaching-resource/Examples-of-Persuasive-Writing-Including-the-War-6179428, published by TSL Education; **p28** Cyber-bullying, NAPLAN Persuasive worksheets – Secondary, adapted from www.blake.com.au/v/vspfiles/assets/images/naplan_sec_persuasive_text_worksheets_download.pdf, reprinted by permission of Blake Publishing; **p31** 'Advantages of the Internet in Education', from www.buzzle.com/articles/advantages-of-the-internet-in-education.html; **p33** Yarrow plant, amended from www.nald.ca/library/learning/academic/english/writing/reports/module11.pdf, published by National Adult Literary Database Inc; 'The Yarrow' from James Orchard Halliwell, *Popular Rhymes and Nursery Tales* (1849); **pp34–35** Papua New Guinea, amended from http://k6.boardofstudies.nsw.au/files/english/k6engsamples_syl.pfd; **p36** Computers instead of teachers, adapted from www.ielts-blog.com/ielts-writing-samples/ielts-essays-band-8/ielts-essay-topic-computers-instead-of-teachers, © Simone Braverman, reproduced by permission of IELTS-Blog.com; **pp40–41** 'Holiday to Thailand', from *Standard Grade Folio 2011*, © Scottish Qualifications Authority; **pp42–43** 'Recording King', from *Intermediate 2 Writing Folio 2012*, © Scottish Qualifications Authority; **pp45–48** 'Brotherly and sisterly love', adapted from *Intermediate 2 Writing Folio 2012*, © Scottish Qualifications Authority; **pp51–52** 'Here I am', adapted from *Intermediate 2 Folio 2012*, © Scottish Qualifications Authority; **p56** 'Glasgow Sonnet 1' from Edwin Morgan, *Collected Poems* (Carcanet Press, 1990), copyright © 1990 Edwin Morgan, reproduced by permission of Carcanet Press Ltd; **p58** 'Glasgow, 5 March 1971' ('With a ragged diamond') from Edwin Morgan, *Collected Poems* (Carcanet Press, 1990), copyright © 1990 Edwin Morgan, reproduced by permission of Carcanet Press Ltd; **p65** The Persistence of Memory, adapted from http://overnightessay.com/blog/2012/04/26/a-descriptive-essay-example-learn-what-makes-a-perfect-writing; **p66** A walk in the park, adapted from http://academichelp.net/samples; **pp69–72** General assessment information, © Scottish Qualifications Authority; **pp73–74** 'Safe beneath the surface', from *Intermediate Folio 2011*, © Scottish Qualifications Authority; **pp76–77** 'Phones for you?', from *Intermediate 2 Folio 2012*, © Scottish Qualifications Authority; **pp78–79** 'Has the game changed?' from *Understanding Standards 2011 Intermediate 2*, © Scottish Qualifications Authority.

All SQA published information is reprinted by kind permission of the Scottish Qualifications Authority.

Every effort has been made to trace all copyright holders, but if any have been inadvertently overlooked the Publishers will be pleased to make the necessary arrangements at the first opportunity.

Although every effort has been made to ensure that website addresses are correct at time of going to press, Hodder Gibson cannot be held responsible for the content of any website mentioned in this book. It is sometimes possible to find a relocated web page by typing in the address of the home page for a website in the URL window of your browser.

Hachette UK's policy is to use papers that are natural, renewable and recyclable products and made from wood grown in sustainable forests. The logging and manufacturing processes are expected to conform to the environmental regulations of the country of origin.

Orders: please contact Bookpoint Ltd, 130 Park Drive, Abingdon, Oxon OX14 4SE. Telephone: (44) 01235 827720; Fax: (44) 01235 400454. Lines are open 9.00–5.00, Monday to Saturday, with a 24-hour message answering service. Visit our website at www.hoddereducation.co.uk. Hodder Gibson can be contacted direct on: Tel: 0141 848 1609; Fax: 0141 889 6315; email: hoddergibson@hodder.co.uk

© Willie McGuire, 2013

First published in 2013 by

Hodder Gibson, an imprint of Hodder Education

An Hachette UK Company

2a Christie Street

Paisley PA1 1NB

Impression number   5 4 3 2 1

Year   2017 2016 2015 2014 2013

All rights reserved. Apart from any use permitted under UK copyright law, no part of this publication may be reproduced or transmitted in any form or by any means, electronic or mechanical, including photocopying and recording, or held within any information storage and retrieval system, without permission in writing from the publisher or under licence from the Copyright Licensing Agency Limited. Further details of such licences (for reprographic reproduction) may be obtained from the Copyright Licensing Agency Limited, Saffron House, 6–10 Kirby Street, London EC1N 8TS.

Cover photo © Alexander Raths – Fotolia.com

Illustrations by Barking Dog Art Design & Illustration and Integra Software Services Pvt. Ltd., Pondicherry, India

Typeset in Minion Regular 12/14.5 by Integra Software Services Pvt. Ltd., Pondicherry, India

Printed in Spain

A catalogue record for this title is available from the British Library

ISBN: 978 1444 187 298

CONTENTS

CHAPTER ONE

INTRODUCTION: WHAT DO I NEED TO KNOW?

The aim of this textbook is to provide you with a resource to help you achieve success in the National 5 English writing portfolio. The portfolio comprises 30 per cent of the marks for National 5 English, which equates to almost a third of the overall marks available for the whole course. In other words, it is well worth working very hard in this area as it **will** help to improve your English grade. You don't know what your close reading examination paper will look like so you have little control over it. Equally, you have no control over the questions that will be chosen for the Textual Analysis and Critical Essay sections. You **do** have control, however, over your portfolio, and this textbook will help you to use this to your advantage.

This book

Chapter 1 tells you the main things you need to know about the portfolio. Chapter 2 then helps you to gather ideas. Chapter 3 goes on to examine broadly discursive models of writing. Chapter 4 then does the same with broadly creative writing forms. Chapter 5 also examines models but this time with the focus on assessment. Chapter 6 shows you how to avoid the key technical problems, and Chapter 7 gives you the answers to the conference calls in Chapter 6!

What is a portfolio?

What kind of writing do I need to include in my portfolio?

Your portfolio is a collection of **two** of your best pieces of writing, which will be sent to the SQA for external assessment.

There are **two** broad forms of writing and you must include **one** piece from **each** of these forms.

The first form is **discursive writing**. This broad category can be broken down into: **conveying information**, **argumentative writing**, **persuasive writing** and **report writing**.

The second broad form of writing is **creative**, which can also be broken down, this time into: **personal/reflective** or **imaginative** (short story, poem or drama script).

The marks

Fifteen marks will be awarded for each piece of writing chosen for the portfolio, making a total of 30 marks or **30 per cent of your overall award.**

How can I make sure I get a good mark? What are the markers looking for?

The rules

Because you are not being asked to produce the portfolio under examination conditions, the SQA provides guidance to schools to ensure that what you submit is, **entirely**, your own work. Your teacher needs to be able to track the progress of your work and you should be able to **demonstrate the writing process**. Usually, this is best achieved through a log.

Planning

The process of constructing a writing piece is circular rather than linear. It starts with a number of ideas. These are then narrowed down to a single topic, which then becomes a title. Once you have a working title, you can consider how best to deal with your topic. This would involve an outline plan of what you might include. Once you have completed this you can begin the first draft of the work, which would then be followed by the final draft.

CHAPTER TWO

GETTING STARTED

Discursive	Creative	Imaginative
Conveying information Here, the purpose of the writing is to communicate specific information clearly and accurately to the reader. With this form of writing, you have a great deal of scope in the selection of the topic.	**Personal/reflective** **Personal** writing concerns your feelings about significant events and your reactions to them. **Reflective** writing adds another dimension to personal writing as it usually involves a change of view on the original event, so it goes beyond describing feelings and reactions alone. For the portfolio, your writing can be **either** personal **or** reflective, **or** can share elements of both.	**Short story** Be wary! This is a very specific writing form that uses key features such as setting, characters and plot to highlight a key theme(s).
Argumentative This form of writing might be discursive, where you argue your side of a particular argument, or you might choose to present a balanced view of the topic. In both cases, however, you must cover at least two points of view. In other words, you must consider the views of someone who would not agree with your argument.		**Poem or group of poems** or **A drama script** or **A chapter from a novel** The possibilities are endless!
Persuasive This kind of writing tries to persuade the reader to your point of view using techniques designed to get them to agree with you other than using evidence and argument alone.		
Report Report writing is about presenting facts from a number of different sources in a clear, logical manner.		

I've got a great idea!

Me too!

What's best for me?

You can't cover all of the writing forms available to you for inclusion in the portfolio so you need to decide which form of writing suits you best. Be careful! This is not always the form you might like to write about. You need to discuss this with your teacher to decide on your strengths. Let's look at some options.

Discursive

Conveying information

Special interests

What are your interests? Here are some ideas to begin your exploration of your own areas of interest.

Now add five more.

-
-
-
-
-

Argumentative

Views

The world changes around us daily and often we will have (very) strong views on those changes. Here are some topics to consider.

Social networking destroys real communication.

Internet: friend not foe.

I can marry and have children, work, leave school, fight for Queen and country, but I have no voice as I can't vote. It can't be right …

Try to add five more.

-
-
-
-
-

Creative and imaginative

These kinds of writing might be about a lot of things. Here are some titles to get you thinking about possible short-story topics.

- A Night to Remember.
- A Chance Meeting.
- In Spite.
- The Illustrator.
- The Last Dance.

Task

Now try to add another five titles to the list. Then consider how you might develop these storylines. The first one is done for you, roughly.

-
-
-
-
-

A Night to Remember

End with the title. Focus is on a celebration. An awards ceremony. A prize-giving. Awarded title of young Scottish musician of the year by the BBC. Description of venue. Don't start at breakfast! Begin at the venue and then describe why I am there. Feelings stated implicitly. Describe other guests. The runners-up. Presenters. Why me? Begin with description of the venue – the Dunblane Hydro hotel. Describe the elegant driveway leading up to the magnificent castle itself. A powdering of snow ...

Important events

Everyone has key moments in their lives. Use the ideas below to build up your own events timeline.

Starting school ...

↓

Birth of brother ...

↓

First trip to cinema ...

↓

↓

↓

↓

↓

Try to add five items to the timeline.

Memories

Some memories are very strong even though they may not be exactly important events. Here are some starters to get you thinking about your own memories.

> Learning to ride a bike.

> Your first swim in the sea.

> A perfect day.

Try to add five more.

-
-
-
-
-

Places

We are often influenced by places. Here are some examples of special places.

> Forest Den

> Mountain Hideaway

> Country Cottage

Try to add five more.

-
-
-
-
-

People

Probably nothing influences us as much as other people, who can play very positive roles in our lives. Here are some ideas.

Try to add five more and also consider why these people have played such an important part in your life.

-
-
-
-
-

Things you need to know

Word limit

One thousand words is the upper **limit**. If you exceed this limit, your work may be referred to the Principal Assessor and **may be penalised**. You should aim to produce pieces of writing at or about 1000 words. This does not mean that if your writing pieces fall below 1000 words that they can't be awarded the highest grades. Writing well under 1000 words, though, can be 'self-penalising', meaning that it is not likely to gain very high marks. Writing pieces under 500 words are likely to be awarded 6/15, with exceptionally weak pieces being awarded 4/15. Marks below 4/15, while possible, are likely to be very rare.

How many words must I write?

Sources

All the main sources consulted must be acknowledged in discursive writing. If no sources have been consulted, this must be stated explicitly. Specific details of sources must be given – for example, dates and writers of newspaper articles, specific web pages, titles and dates of publication of books. It is not acceptable to say, for example, 'various newspaper articles' or 'environmental websites' or 'the Internet'.

Any direct quotations from sources must be clearly acknowledged by the use of quotation marks. Unacknowledged use of others' material, such as copying and pasting from the Internet or any other source, or re-wording or summarising information from another source and passing it off as your own without acknowledging its source, is plagiarism, and this carries severe penalties!

What do I do?

Writing it right

The pieces of writing in the portfolio must be produced under conditions that ensure the work is your own. You may need to sign a declaration that the work in the portfolio is your own and that you were unassisted other than by legitimate support from, for example, a teacher or lecturer (see 'What is unacceptable?' opposite). The pieces of writing must be unassisted **at the time of writing** and produced under a system of supervision that guarantees authenticity through a process requiring you to submit the following at appropriate stages:

Stage 1: draft title and
proposals as well as
outline plan

↓

Stage 2: writing

↓

What help can I get?

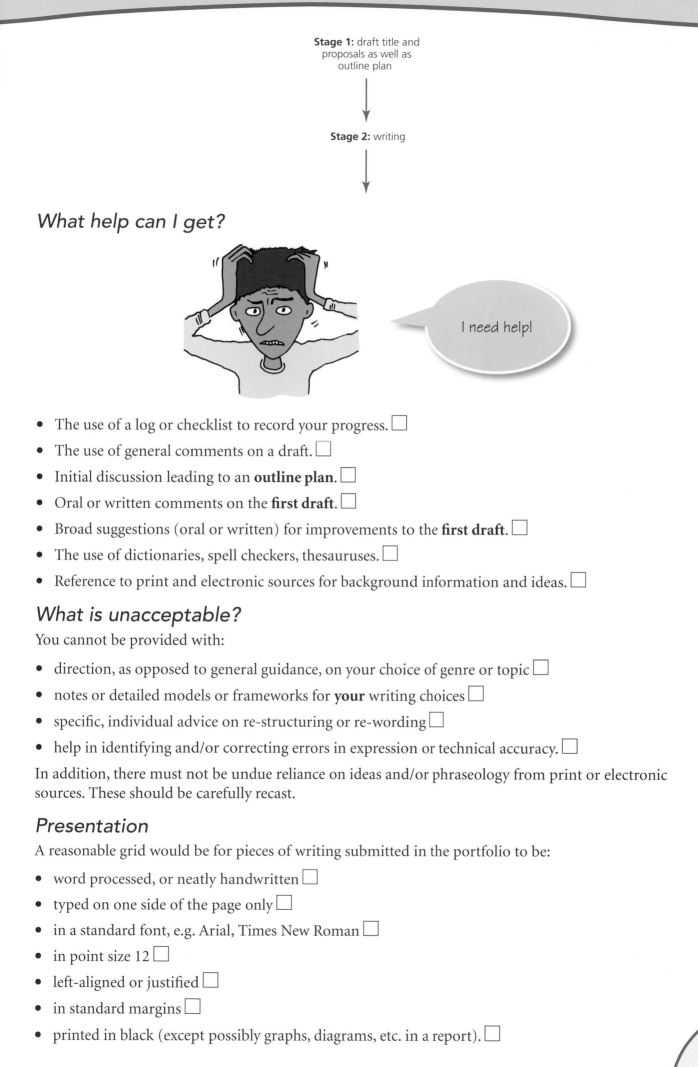

I need help!

- The use of a log or checklist to record your progress. ☐
- The use of general comments on a draft. ☐
- Initial discussion leading to an **outline plan**. ☐
- Oral or written comments on the **first draft**. ☐
- Broad suggestions (oral or written) for improvements to the **first draft**. ☐
- The use of dictionaries, spell checkers, thesauruses. ☐
- Reference to print and electronic sources for background information and ideas. ☐

What is unacceptable?

You cannot be provided with:

- direction, as opposed to general guidance, on your choice of genre or topic ☐
- notes or detailed models or frameworks for **your** writing choices ☐
- specific, individual advice on re-structuring or re-wording ☐
- help in identifying and/or correcting errors in expression or technical accuracy. ☐

In addition, there must not be undue reliance on ideas and/or phraseology from print or electronic sources. These should be carefully recast.

Presentation

A reasonable grid would be for pieces of writing submitted in the portfolio to be:

- word processed, or neatly handwritten ☐
- typed on one side of the page only ☐
- in a standard font, e.g. Arial, Times New Roman ☐
- in point size 12 ☐
- left-aligned or justified ☐
- in standard margins ☐
- printed in black (except possibly graphs, diagrams, etc. in a report). ☐

CHAPTER THREE

DISCURSIVE WRITING
CONVEYING INFORMATION

What's that all about?

Writing that conveys information should have a clear purpose and may well be written in a specific genre. A feature article for a specialist magazine on car modification, for example, is likely to use the 'language' of such magazines: 'ECU … power curve … dump valves'.

Remember that part of the craft in conveying information is also to maintain the reader's attention and, for this reason, what you write must be presented in an **interesting** and **engaging** way. You may wish to add to the attractiveness of your writing by adding graphics, diagrams and/or images.

The style of the writing, too, can help to **entertain** and maintain the reader's attention throughout, if it is lively, informative, interesting and engaging.

Writing based on providing information about a topic should not be simply a series of lifts from different magazines; you should try to make the writing your own. A review of two online blogs on the topic of Internet privacy, for example, should clearly use sentence construction, a structure and word choices that are not identical (or nearly identical) to the sources.

What are its features?

- Gives information about a topic.
- May use technical or specialised vocabulary.
- De-personalised style, written in the third person (he/she/it).
- Formal tone.
- Avoidance of emotions.
- Avoidance of prosaic language.
- Use of time connectives, e.g. initially, next, finally, subsequently, firstly, afterwards, at last, once, secondly, in the end, eventually.

How is it shaped?

- The subject is often stated in the opening paragraph.
- Follows a logical structure under headings or sub-headings, or is centred on specific themes or issues.
- Use of diagrams/illustrations.
- A conclusion rounds off the text.
- The **subject** and **purpose** of the writing are both clearly stated.

Sample

Car modification

Car modification has been growing in popularity for many years, perhaps because of the increasing cost of owning prestige vehicles. As such, 'mods' are often seen as a relatively inexpensive way of transforming a basic car into something of which the owner can be proud. The purpose, then, of this article is to convey information about the various forms of car modification and how they might improve the car ownership experience.

Cluster similar ideas/points

Mind maps

Mind maps are helpful to gather initial ideas together. Here's a worked example based on car modification:

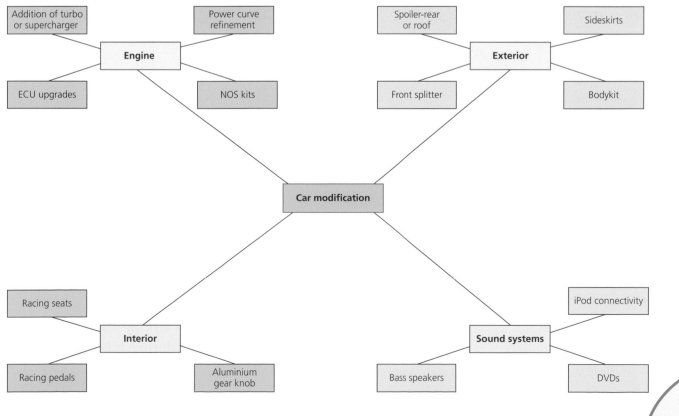

Online software called **bubbl.us** will create a mind map for you.

- https://bubbl.us

Choose a topic in which you are interested and then try it out!

Concept maps

Concept maps are like mind maps, but they show the relationship between the different items. Below is a worked example, again, on car modification:

The online software **Edraw** provides you with free concept mapping.

- www.edrawsoft.com/concept-mapping-software.php

Once you have looked at the example below, try to change your chosen topic into a concept map.

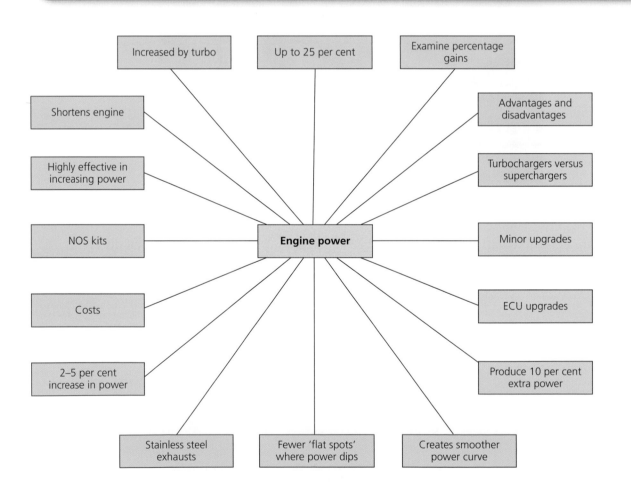

In writing that conveys information:

- language may be technical, for example ECU, power curve

- the third person narrative mode is used, for example 'this article'

- personal feelings are avoided, for example not 'I think car mods are brilliant!'

- there is logical sequencing of ideas. One of the problems in this form of writing is how to organise the material. Try to use clear linking words, such as first, then, during, however, despite, similarly.

Task

Work in pairs to produce a list of five more linking words.

Research

Many people make the mistake of attempting to produce this form of writing without the appropriate research. Researching your topic is just as important in this form of writing as it is in discursive writing if you want to write knowledgeably. Remember that you must have information to communicate in order to succeed!

The web search

The first step here is to select appropriate **keywords**. Keywords are search terms and they define how wide or how tight the search will be; these are known as **search parameters**. The keywords 'snowboarding' or 'snowboarding information' will give you a huge list of hits, but this will present you with a problem – how to refine the range of materials. You might try searching 'snowboarding equipment' to narrow the range, or 'snowboarding origins' for background information.

It is also important that you attempt to validate your sources. 'Billy's Blog' on snowboarding, for example, might contain all sorts of interesting information, but is it accurate? It might be less accurate than information on Wikipedia, which itself might be less accurate than something appearing on a specialist website. The key is to use **triangulation**, where you try to **validate** your **data** using other sites.

Before you attempt the topic below, try to do a search for the topic of snowboarding. **What are your results?**

Mini research project – homework activity 1

Now you are going to practise your research skills. Scan the three snowboarding websites below, then answer the questions.

Snowboarding
- http://en.wikipedia.org/wiki/Snowboarding
- www.abc-of-snowboarding.com/info
- http://snowboarding.about.com/od/snowboardequipment/u/EquipmentTab.htm

Questions

1. Which website is likely to be the most helpful?
2. Why?

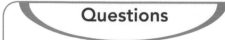

Now scan the three horse-riding sites below and then answer the questions.

Horse riding

- www.equine-world.co.uk/riding_horses/index.asp
- www.horseridingbreconbeacons.com
- www.nationaltrail.co.uk/Peddarsway/uploads/Horse%20Riding%20information%20 sheet%20v4(3).pdf

Questions

1. Which one of these sources is likely to give you the most **general** information on the topic?
2. What is wrong with the other two sources?
3. How do you now go about drawing out the information you need?

Finally, scan the gaming sites below and then answer the questions.

Computer gaming

- http://en.wikipedia.org/wiki/Computer_gaming
- http://ezgamerz.com
- www.gamesradar.com/all-platforms/news
- www.infotoday.com/cilmag/may06/Doshi.shtml
- http://freeola.com/wireless-broadband-network/online-gaming.php

Questions

1. Which one of these sources is likely to give you the most general information on the topic?
2. Why would you reject the other sources?
3. How do you now go about drawing out the information you need?

How will you now manage your research?

You now need to organise your ideas to give them a structure. Let's scan this web page to demonstrate:

http://en.wikipedia.org/wiki/Snowboarding

There's a lot of information on this page. Are you going to simply copy all of this information into a Word document? This might take you over the word limit. What you need to do is organise what you need for your article. Let's imagine you have chosen the topic of snowboarding. Here are some suggested headings:

- Definition
- A (brief) history of snowboarding

Now read the web page above, then write down the key points you might wish to include:

- equipment required and costs
- safety
- styles
- competitions
- growing popularity in the media.

The history of snowboarding

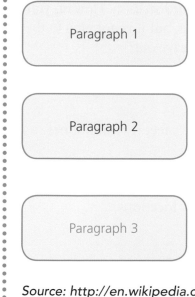

Snowboarding has been around since the 1920s, when boys and men would tie plywood or wooden planks from barrels to their feet with clotheslines and use horse reins in order to steer themselves down hills.

Modern snowboarding began in 1965 when Sherman Poppen, an engineer in Muskegon, Michigan, invented a toy for his daughter by fastening two skis together and attaching a rope to one end so she would have some control as she stood on the board and glided downhill.

Dubbed the 'snurfer' (combining snow and surfer), the toy proved so popular among his daughter's friends that Poppen licensed the idea to a manufacturer that sold about a million snurfers over the next decade. Over half a million snurfers were sold in 1966 alone.

Source: http://en.wikipedia.org/wiki/Snowboarding

Now you need to **summarise** the key points. Let's look at the opening paragraph.

Note-making versus note-taking

To communicate information effectively, you need to research your topic. To do this, you need to read about it. When you read an article, you often have to decide on the main pieces of information you will include in your own writing. This means that you will be accepting some bits of information and rejecting others. You will also be changing the way in which the information is written. You can't simply copy the article and pass it off as your own work. That would be plagiarism. Here's how to avoid it.

Avoiding plagiarism

Note-taking is about noting down information. Here are some of the main ideas from paragraph 1 in the box above:

Snowboarding invented 1920s … men and boys … plywood or wooden planks from barrels … tied to feet … used clotheslines and horse reins for steering … downhill … modern event 1965 … Sherman Poppen … engineer … Michigan … toy for daughter … skis … rope … control … called snurfer … snow+surfer … licensed idea … sold a million … sales picked up quickly.

Note-making is then about deciding what to reject, what to keep, and then **creating your own notes**:

Snowboarding invented 1920s. Equipment basic. Wood tied to feet. Used horse reins for steering.

From note-making to key points

You now need to turn your notes into formal continuous English.

Key point 1

The early origins of snowboarding began in the 1920s, although the equipment was very basic, using pieces of wood tied to the feet and horse reins for steering.

Key point 2

The modern sport began in 1965 with the invention of the 'snurfer', essentially a combination of two skis tied together, with a rope attached for steering.

A lot of the information in the original is helpful, but you are going to have to write a comprehensive piece telling your audience about snowboarding in no more than 1000 words if you choose this topic for the next homework activity. To do this, you have to **summarise** key information. How do you do this? Let's look more closely. Much of the information given is interesting, but it is not vital to the task of conveying information about the sport in general. What can we leave out?

Summarising is about leaving out information that isn't vital. What can we leave out?

Paragraph 1

Leave out references to: boys and men … plywood … planks … barrels … feet … clotheslines … down hills.

Paragraph 2

Leave out references to: names … occupations … family relationships … locations … explanations … marketing the product … product sales.

Your turn

Try to remove from the extract below everything that is not required. Remember that you are trying to give general, not specific, information about snowboarding.

In the early 1970s, Poppen organised snurfing competitions at a Michigan ski resort that attracted enthusiasts from all over the country. One of those early pioneers was Tom Sims, a devotee of skateboarding (a sport born in the 1950s, when kids attached roller skate wheels to small boards that they steered by shifting their weight). As an eighth grader in Haddonfield, New Jersey, in the 1960s, Sims crafted a snowboard in his school shop class by gluing carpet to the top of a piece of wood and attaching aluminium sheeting to the bottom. He produced commercial snowboards in the mid- '70s. ➜

During this same time, Dimitrije Milovich – an American surfing enthusiast who had also enjoyed sliding down snowy hills on caféteria trays during his college years in upstate New York – constructed a snowboard called 'Winterstick', inspired by the design and feel of a surfboard. Articles about his invention in such mainstream magazines as *Newsweek* helped publicise the young sport.

Task

Now make notes on the paragraph you have written.
Decide what to keep and what to reject.

Note-making

Make your own notes on the main ideas.

Now convert your notes into key points:

* Key point 1:

* Key point 2:

* Key point 3:

Mini research project – homework activity 4

Now select **one** of the topics (snowboarding, computer gaming or horse-riding) and write an account of it in 1000 words.

Possible topics for conveying information

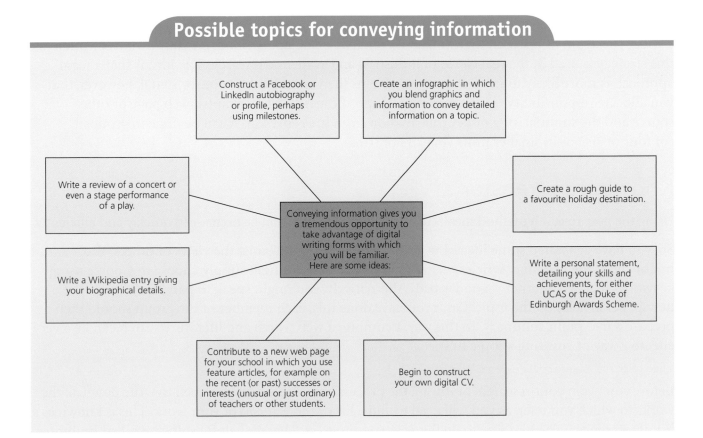

Construct a Facebook or LinkedIn autobiography or profile, perhaps using milestones.

Create an infographic in which you blend graphics and information to convey detailed information on a topic.

Write a review of a concert or even a stage performance of a play.

Conveying information gives you a tremendous opportunity to take advantage of digital writing forms with which you will be familiar. Here are some ideas:

Create a rough guide to a favourite holiday destination.

Write a Wikipedia entry giving your biographical details.

Write a personal statement, detailing your skills and achievements, for either UCAS or the Duke of Edinburgh Awards Scheme.

Contribute to a new web page for your school in which you use feature articles, for example on the recent (or past) successes or interests (unusual or just ordinary) of teachers or other students.

Begin to construct your own digital CV.

ARGUMENTATIVE

We have already looked at one form of search, the web search. Helpful as this is, there are also other ways of finding out information about a topic.

Literature search

This allows you to source information from books, journals, newspapers, magazines, specialist publications and encyclopedias.

This can, however, take a **lot** of time and needs to be planned carefully.

It is also well worth consulting the school/college librarian to assist you with your search.

Selecting a topic

The Internet? We'd be better off without it.

What do you think?

Task

Work in groups of four to generate ideas/views/opinions.
Here are a few to help you:

Yes, we would!

- It takes up too much of our time.
- It stops people from studying.
- It distracts us from 'real' life.

No, we wouldn't!

- It gives fast access to knowledge.
- It helps us study.
- It **is** real life. It's how we live now.

Peer research

This allows you to solve some of the time problems mentioned earlier and also enables you to cover a wider spectrum of research than you could otherwise manage working on your own. Very often this strategy is used in the real world of industrial and academic research. The idea is that a team approach is more likely to solve complex problems than an individual one. It is vital, however, that you allocate responsibility for the reading of a specific article, book chapter, web page or other source and the summarising of key information from it. Peer research can be done in groups (of four or six) or in smaller units (in pairs or trios).

Knowledge transfer

Using the peer research method means that lots of information can be exchanged quickly and efficiently.

So, you have generated some ideas, but you need to test these against the views of others. You might check the Essential Articles* series, if available, or you might simply choose to Google using keywords such as 'Internet + good + bad'. Alternatively, you might speak to parents or even read newspaper articles on the topic. Once you have done this, each member of the group should then prepare a five-point summary. In this way, a combined web search and literature search can be a very effective way of covering a topic fully.

* See http://carelpress.co.uk/essentialarticles

Before you begin your research, or during the process, remember that you need to write down all the works to which you refer, as you will need to add a list of these at end of your work. This is known as a list of **references**. The best way to do this is as you progress. There is helpful software called **Endnotes** and even a tool in Microsoft Word that will create reference lists (see the box at the top of page 23).

Homework activity 5

Online tutorial

Watch the following online tutorial. It takes you through the process step by step.

- www.youtube.com/watch?v=X1q5zMdUf3g

Endnotes tool

Now try the tool itself.

- http://office.microsoft.com/en-gb/word-help/insert-a-footnote-or-an-endnote-HP005230226.aspx

Task

Ordering ideas	Evidence
Key point 1:	
Key point 2:	
Key point 3:	
Key point 4:	
Key point 5:	

You should now be in a position where you can begin to order your ideas.

What are the strongest arguments in favour of the Internet? What are the weakest? How will you conclude?

Planning the response

There are a number of plans you might use. Two possible plans are shown below.

Version 1: For and against

Part 1

- Introduces the topic to the reader, outlines why it is important and indicates your (the writer's) point of view.

Part 2

- Introduces five key arguments **supporting** your point of view using Point. Evidence. Explain.

Websites

See the links below for online tutorials.

- www.teacher-of-literacy.com/point,-evidence,-explain-teaching-resources-432
- www.bbc.co.uk/bitesize/ks3/english/reading/character/revision/6

Part 3

- Introduces five key arguments **against** your point of view.

Part 4

- **Concludes** the piece by re-stating your point of view.

Version 2: The 'integrated' plan

Brings together **both** sides of an argument in the same paragraph and **argues** them through; in other words they are balanced against each other so the reader can **evaluate** the **development** of each argument.

- Paragraph 1: introduces the topic to the reader, outlines why it is important and indicates the writer's point of view.

Sample

The Internet is one of the most famous (or infamous) artefacts in the world. It is hard to ignore and, some would argue, even impossible to avoid in daily life. Is it a good thing, though? Obviously, this question generates emotional responses either in the negative or the affirmative. My inclination is towards the latter – it is certainly a good thing.

- Paragraph 2: opposing viewpoint 1. First argument opposing the writer's viewpoint **and** counterargument 1.

Sample

Some would argue that the Internet is a very bad thing, citing a variety of arguments. One such argument is that Internet use simply takes up too much of our time and is, therefore, clearly unhealthy. Is this, however, an entirely valid assumption to draw? A report by Hexus states that, 'The largest proportion of Internet users [was] in the youngest age group (those aged 16–24), at 98.7 per cent. This represents 7.18 million people.' And that's a lot of young people! Not only is the quantity important, though, so too is the quality of many of those online interactions, as many young people use the fast knowledge available to them to learn more quickly, efficiently and independently.

Source: http://hexus.net/ce/news/internet/35265-uk-internet-usage-report-16-adults-havent-online

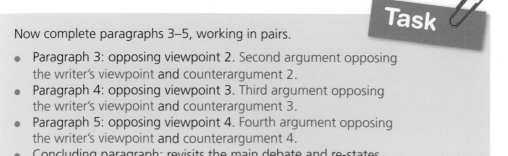

Task

Now complete paragraphs 3–5, working in pairs.

- Paragraph 3: opposing viewpoint 2. Second argument opposing the writer's viewpoint and counterargument 2.
- Paragraph 4: opposing viewpoint 3. Third argument opposing the writer's viewpoint and counterargument 3.
- Paragraph 5: opposing viewpoint 4. Fourth argument opposing the writer's viewpoint and counterargument 4.
- Concluding paragraph: revisits the main debate and re-states the writer's point of view.

Line of thought

Using a plan helps to preserve your **line of thought**, which is the **overall direction** in which your thoughts or arguments are going. This should be consistent. If you are arguing, for example, that the Internet is a bad thing, this should be the case all through the writing. You cannot become confused and start arguing that it is a good thing! Even when you are presenting the opposing viewpoint, you are doing this simply to argue against it.

Sources: primary and secondary

Remember that you **must** acknowledge **all the sources you have used** in your writing. These can be **primary** sources, which are original accounts, or **secondary** sources, where someone else has interpreted the primary source.

One easy way both to deal with sources and to avoid plagiarism is to use the system below.

Sources are written **in the text** of your assignment by citing the author's surname followed by the date of the source in brackets:

Cunningham (2010)

These sources will also form your **reference list** and need to be presented in alphabetical order by author name (and not the order in which they appear in the essay) at the end of the writing, where the citation would now look like this:

Cunningham, C. (2010) English Made Easy.

This web resource might also help you to organise your sources; it does it all for you! Remember that when referring to **websites**, you need to add when you last accessed them, as you can see below:

www.neilstoolbox.com/bibliography-creator/reference-website.htm (last accessed 4.5.13)

Task

Choose **ONE** of these topics or one of your own.

- **Research** the topic.
- Then create **either** a version 1 **or** a version 2 **plan** for it.
- Finally, **write** the argumentative essay, using your plan.

Possible argumentative topics

- We have become a society obsessed by weight.
- TV shows such as *The X Factor* and *Britain's Got Talent* have discouraged young people from finding success through hard work.
- Technology creates many benefits for society, but there is a high price to pay for them.
- The older generation has really messed things up for the young.
- Money. Money. Money. It's all we think or care about today.

- As a society, we have become less caring.
- Virtual learning environments (VLEs), such as Moodle, Edmodo and GLOW, are changing the way we learn for the better.
- Teenagers must not allow the economic climate to get them down. They must become more involved in politics.
- With obesity among the young becoming a huge problem, it is time we looked at alternatives to our usual diet. Flexitarianism is the way forward.

Websites

These websites might prove useful when you are researching topics.

- www.homeworktips.about.com/od/essaywriting/a/argumenttopics.html
- http://misslindsayenglish.wordpress.com (go to Discursive Writing category)
- http://cumnockacademy-links.wikispaces.com (go to Discursive Essay topics in the English section)
- www.misterconnor.com/2010/06/higher-discursive-writing-topics.html (does say 'Higher', but many topics would work equally well for National 5)

PERSUASIVE

What is persuasive writing?

The aim of persuasive writing is to persuade the reader towards the writer's adopted **point of view** or **purpose**. It can take many forms, from advertising to political speeches and even sales pitches. Often, when the writing is effective, this can influence a reader's beliefs or opinions. It usually focuses on a single topic or issue and it will carry a sense of conviction, commitment or belief by manipulating language to create an appropriate tone. It may also use some or all of the following genre characteristics: manipulating key information; the deliberate omission of opposing evidence; flattery; claiming exclusivity or necessity; making appeals to reason; and employing technical jargon/rhetoric or repetition. It is very like discursive writing, but unlike discursive writing it attempts to persuade us to a point of view by an appeal to the emotions, as opposed to the use of reason and argument alone.

What are its features?

- Can be either formal or informal
- Imperatives
- Exaggeration
- Figurative language
- Emotional language
- Can be in the first person
- Repetition
- Rhetorical questions
- Flattery
- Linking words, e.g. consequently, because, as such, therefore, subsequently
- Uses facts emotively
- Omission of opposing viewpoints.

Uses modal verbs – for example could, can, may, might, will, would, shall, should, must – to convey a judgement about the likelihood of something happening. **Must** is more likely to be used than **should**, and **will** rather than **might**, because these words carry a higher degree of certainty.

How is it shaped?

- **The opening statement** will put across the main point of view.
- **The main text** will give either opinions supported by facts or facts supported by opinions, but the language devices mentioned above will feature strongly in persuading the reader towards the main point of view.
- **The conclusion** will summarise and re-state the opening position and sum up the issues.

A work in progress

Read the piece below. It shows a piece of work in the early stages of development, and will give you an idea of some of the main features of persuasive writing.

Visit Hong Kong

Question and answer structure.
Justifies why Hong Kong is so good and lists its special qualities.

Inverted commas.
Derogatory. Belittles the 'so called' or not authentic Chinese restaurants in England. Those in Hong Kong are obviously the real thing!

Emotional language.
'Amazed … magnificent … fabulous …'
Avoiding the negatives. None of the downsides is mentioned.

Rhetorical questions.
'Do you want?' and 'Do you want to be missing?' warn against missing out on something unique.

Use of imperatives.
'Try … Visit … Go …'

Emotional appeal.
'If you are prepared to miss this fabulous experience, then you must be completely out of your mind!'

Do you want to miss out on a once-in-a-lifetime experience? If not, then visit Hong Kong! Full of Oriental landmarks, temples and shops, Hong Kong is one of the most traditional places in the world. Try dim sum, the Chinese food style, dating back centuries, which tastes unlike anything in the 'Chinese' restaurants in England. Do you want to miss out? Visit the jade market, the best jewellery centre ever, selling pearls, gem stones, china ornaments and much more, or the temples, where you can marvel at the magnificent architecture. Visit Victoria Peak, a magnificent mountain, and be amazed by the beautiful views. Do you want to be missing this incredible experience?

Go on the Star Ferry, from Kowloon to Hong Kong Island, or visit Macau, the Portuguese island, and go bungee jumping on famous (and enormous) Macau Tower! If you are prepared to miss this fabulous experience, then you must be completely out of your mind!

Source: http://www.tes.co.uk/teaching-resource/ Examples-of-Persuasive-Writing-Including-the- War-6179428

Write down **TWO** strengths of this piece and **TWO** development needs.

Now read the following piece.

Cyber-bullying

Cyber-bullying is an ever-increasing problem faced by many people today. Research shows that the majority of students in the UK today have been targeted by cyber-bullies. Fortunately, there are a number of strategies we can use to ensure that cyber-bullies don't succeed in their efforts.

To disarm cyber-bullies, make sure you don't give them any ammunition against you or your friends. This means that you should never write, send or publish anything that could be used as a weapon to embarrass, threaten or discredit you. This includes written messages, photos, video or audio recordings.

A simple rule to remember is not to say or share anything online about other people that you wouldn't be prepared to say to them or show them in person. Better still, if you make a comment about someone else, try to make sure that it is positive. It's never a good idea to bad-mouth others.

Another simple strategy is to ensure that you never send denigrating, threatening, angry, abusive or obscene messages to anyone. It is all too easy to fight back with the same weapons used against you – but all this does is transform you into the bully. Don't play into the real bullies' hands by letting your anger get the better of you!

A third idea that has proven very successful is to inform the authorities about cyber-bullying as soon as it becomes apparent that you are being targeted. If you or a person you know is being bullied online, simply tell someone about it. A bully's power is undermined when their clandestine activities are exposed to public scrutiny. This also shows the bully that you cannot be intimidated into keeping quiet. There are many people out there who can help, including parents, teachers and friends.

Fighting cyber-bullies can also occur at home. Some basic rules can be put into place within the family structure. Parents' expectations about their children's online activities should be made clear before Internet access is provided at home. Parents should also place computers in less private areas of the house, so that online interactions can be monitored from a respectful distance.

It is also important to consider that cyber-bullies aren't all that different from old-fashioned bullies. Many are crying out for attention and care. So we must offer them help, care and concern. A bully may be facing emotional problems that cause this behaviour. Speaking out about cyber-bullying can assist the bullies themselves, not just their victims.

Although cyber-bullying has been made possible through hi-tech telecommunications machinery, it can really only be prevented by people: good relationships, genuine care for others and open communication are our best defences.

Source: NAPLAN Persuasive Text sample worksheets – Secondary (adapted)

Working in pairs, complete the grid.

Technique	Quotation	Effect
Reference to statistics		Suggests arguments made are valid
Second person		
Imperatives	Don't play	
Emotional appeal	Victims	
Statement/answer		
Exclamation marks		
Second person	You	

Possible persuasive topics

- The youth of today has more to offer society than the older generation.
- There is too much pressure on young people to succeed academically; there are other ways to succeed.
- Social networking makes us less social in the real world.
- As a society, we have become less interested in religion and this is a good/bad thing.
- Tattoos are very bad idea.
- The age of consent should be the same as the voting age.
- We have every reason to be optimistic/pessimistic about our future.
- Young people today are unfairly/quite rightly portrayed by the media.
- We depend too much on technology. If it failed, then ...
- There is too much emphasis on one side of achievement in schools – the academic. What about sport, music, drama, or developing entrepreneurs?
- More has to be done to prevent the collapse of the high street.
- More has to be done to encourage the use of digital media in schools, including mobile phones.

Task

Choose **ONE** of the topics above **or** one of your own and then write a 500-word piece using the **key features** of persuasive writing.

REPORT

Reports convey information about a particular topic. This information usually needs to have been drawn from **at least** two sources.

Guidelines

A successful report **should**:

- contain **information relevant** to the chosen topic/issue

- be drawn from at **least two** sources

- **recast** and **paraphrase** the source material appropriately according to the purpose of the report

- fulfil a clearly expressed **purpose** and start with a clear statement of that purpose

- carry a **point of view** or **tone** that will depend on the nature of the remit, although this is likely to be **detached** and **objective**

- have an **effective** and **appropriate** structure that should clearly identify the main parts of the report and how they are linked.

It also **may**:

- use charts, graphs, tables and diagrams to enhance the meaning/purposes of the report

- use headings/sub-headings, appendices and lettering or numbering systems to structure the work and to separate the main parts.

What does it look like?	How is it shaped?
Present tense	Begins with a clear outline of what the topic is about, i.e. the remit/purpose
Subject-specific vocabulary or technical/specialised word choices	Headings/sub-headings
Definitions	No irrelevant material
Logical	Information is organised to reflect the main points of the report
Objective stance using third person	Follows a logical sequence
Use of the passive voice	Uses logical connectives (then, consequently, as a result, because)
Detached tone	
Formal language	
Logical connectives (like, therefore, alternatively, as a result, consequently, accordingly)	

Online learning

For the following activities you need access to computers.

Sample topic

We will begin with the sample topic:

The advantages and disadvantages of the Internet in education.

Research – advantages

To write about the topic in a knowledgeable way, you need to find out more about it. To help, go to www.buzzle.com/articles/advantages-of-the-internet-in-education.html.

You are given a number of pieces of information under the following headings.

- Use of Internet in education
- Easy contact
- Projects
- Encyclopedia
- News

Form one group for each heading. Note all the advantages you can think of under each heading. Then carousel, where you share notes – so that each group should deal with each topic.

Homework activity 6

For homework you should write a short report on the advantages and disadvantages of the Internet. To help you with this, carry out the activities below.

Research

To write about this topic in a balanced way, you need to find out more about the disadvantages of the Internet. To help you with your research, go to:

http://answers.yahoo.com/question/index?qid=20080712022042AARzWim

Here you are given more advantages as well as **ten disadvantages**.

Note down the added advantages and the disadvantages.

Planning the writing

You now know something about the topic and are ready to plan your essay. Here's a straightforward plan:

1. Introduction to topic
2. Advantages
3. Disadvantages
4. Conclusion: does one outweigh the other?

Summarising the main ideas

One of the skills of report writing is to summarise the main ideas being presented.

Take the first point in the advantages section:

The Internet is the largest set of computer networks that use the Internet Protocol. The invention and development of the Internet was one of the biggest discoveries by mankind in the twentieth century. Today, the Internet is used by more than 50 per cent of the world's population as its applications are found in nearly every field of life, be it communication, knowledge, news, shopping, marketing, entertainment or education. So how exactly does it benefit students' education? Let us take a look in detail.

Source: www.buzzle.com/articles/advantages-of-the-internet-in-education.html

What are the key facts (as presented by the author)?

1. Used by 50 per cent of the world's population.
2. Used in many areas of our lives, for example communication, learning, news, shopping.
3. What are its benefits?

Task

Summarise the remainder of the advantages article.

You then have the opposite problem with the disadvantages website, as here you have to join the short sentences into formal, connected writing.

Examples of short sentences

- 'There is a lot of wrong information on the Internet. Anyone can post anything, and much of it is garbage.'

- 'There are predators [who] hang out on the Internet waiting to get unsuspecting people [into] dangerous situations.'

Source: http://answers.yahoo.com/question/index?qid=20080712022042AARzWim

Example of formal continuous writing

One of the main disadvantages of the Internet in education is that often it is difficult to determine the accuracy of information there as the checks and balances used to moderate materials published by respected publishing houses are not always followed. Another central concern relates to the safety of children while using the Internet as it is not unknown for adults to use it as a way of meeting children offline.

Task

Now complete a short report (500 words) on the advantages and disadvantages of the Internet.

A work in progress

Now we will look at the **beginning** of a piece of report writing.

Sample topic

Write a report on herbal medicines.

Herbal remedies

With today's fast food 'squat and snaffle' eating patterns, more and more busy people are complaining of gas, indigestion, heartburn and stomach troubles. The best answer might be to change their eating habits, but that isn't always possible in today's fast-paced world. Instead they swallow name-brand antacids and hope for some relief. There is another option, however.

Herbal medicine has been part of human life for thousands of years and it still offers us many health benefits, especially for those looking for an effective treatment for indigestion. Various parts of plants may be processed or an oil may be distilled from them, which can then be used for a variety of medicines.

Yarrow is a good example of a common plant that has healing properties. It has a rough, angular stem with many long, narrow leaves, which have a feathery appearance. The plant flowers in July and August and produces white or pale lilac flowers that look like tiny daisies. It is widely available as, according to Duff, 'Yarrow grows in Britain, Scandinavia, Europe, and all over the United States except for the extreme south.' Most people think of it as a weed because it is often found along the edges of fields or along country roads, but it grows well anywhere that grass will grow. You may not recognise the name 'Yarrow', but it is also called Milfoil, Soldier's Woundwort or Devil's Plaything, and it has been used for centuries to make an ointment for wounds. Legend has it that Achilles used it to stop his soldiers' bleeding wounds during the Trojan Wars. During the Middle Ages, it was thought that it would bring a dream vision of a future husband or wife if wrapped in a flannel cloth and placed under the pillow, while repeating the words:

Thou pretty herb of Venus' tree,

Thy true name it is Yarrow;

Now who my bosom friend must be,

Pray tell thou me to-morrow.

Source: www.nald.ca/library/learning/academic/english/writing/reports/module11.pdf (p.41) (amended)

The piece of writing on the previous page has potential, but it is far from complete.

Work in pairs to discuss and note the strengths of the piece of writing.
How would you improve it? What else is required to develop it?

Strengths	Development needs

A work in progress

Here is another example of a piece of **report writing** in the **process of development**.

Sample topic

Write a report highlighting the key geographical features of Papua New Guinea.

Papua New Guinea

Location

Geographically, Guinea is situated close to Australia, a few kilometres south of the Equator. It forms the end of a long string of islands trailing down from Thailand. Papua New Guinea itself consists of the eastern half of the island of New Guinea as well as a number of smaller islands surrounding the mainland and, unusually, it is surrounded by three seas: the Solomon Sea, the Coral Sea and the Bismarck Sea.

➡

Landforms

It is a very rugged country with parts that have, just recently, been visited by outsiders for the first time and it is divided into north and south regions by a central range of mountains that is 2400 km long.

The largest rivers flowing south are the Fly as well as the Purari and the largest rivers flowing north are the Sepik and the Ramu. Rivers in this country are a means of both transport and communication.

On the coast, there is a swamp-like land formed by a delta of streams, and towards the foothills there are small plains of rich soil. Towards the higher elevations are rugged mountain slopes covered in dense, thick forest until, ultimately, we reach the snow-capped peaks.

There are still a few live volcanoes on the north coast of New Britain, the largest island in Papua New Guinea. The reason for the large number of volcanoes is that this island is on the Ring of Fire, which is where two continental plates (the Pacific and the Australian) push together, thus forcing up the land, which creates a great amount of pressure underneath. These volcanoes, which can be very destructive, can also be of great benefit, for often they bring up rich pumice from deep underground and their eruptions spread it over the land, creating new life from the old.

Climate

The island is hot, humid and wet nearly all year round in some places, but in others there are very distinct changes of wet and dry seasons. The driest place on the island is its capital, Port Moresby, which receives only 1000 mm of rainfall annually, whereas other areas, like the south coast of New Britain and Bougainville Island, can receive up to 9000 mm annually. The coastal temperature varies from 25 to 30°C whereas, in the highlands, it gets so cold that ice forms on some of the highest peaks …

Source: http://k6.boardofstudies.nsw.edu.au/files/english/k6engsamples_syl.pdf (p.134) (amended)

This piece of writing is longer than the former and also shows us the beginnings of a reasonable piece of report writing, but, again, it is far from complete.

Task

Work in pairs to discuss the strengths of this piece of writing. How would you improve it? What else is required to develop it?

Strengths	Development needs

A work in progress

Write a report on the topic of computers replacing teachers in the classroom.

Here is a final example of a piece of **report writing**, again in the **process of development**, but this time much closer to portfolio-readiness.

Computers? I prefer teachers

There is no doubt that education and the learning process have changed since the introduction of computers. The search for information has become easier and connectivity has made data more available to all. Though computers have become more intelligent, they have not yet become a substitute for the human interaction that is so important in the learning process; so what can be expected in the future is a change in the teachers' role, but not their disappearance from the classroom.

Nobody can argue that the acquisition of knowledge is now more fun and easier with computers. The mere activity of touching and exploring this device constitutes an enjoyable task for many learners. This, accompanied by the relaxing attitude and software interactivity, usually contributes to a better grasping of new knowledge. Equally, the availability of digital books, virtual learning environments and other materials provides the student with an ever accessible source of information, that otherwise would not be on hand.

But, besides the increasing complexity of so-called intelligent software, the need for human interaction in the learning process will always be present, at least for the foreseeable future. There is the necessity for a human being to determine the specific needs of each individual. The expertise of a teacher in how to explain and adapt complex concepts to different individuals can hardly be mimicked by a computer, no matter how sophisticated its software is.

As computers are becoming a common tool for teaching, teachers should be more aware of their role as guides in the acquisition of knowledge rather than transmitters of facts. They have to be open-minded to the changes that are taking place, keep updated and serve as problem solvers in the learning process, thus allowing students to discover the facts for themselves.

To summarise, teachers play and will continue to play an important role in the classroom. No matter how complex computers become, there will be no replacement for the human interaction, but maybe in the way in which this interaction takes place.

Source: www.ielts-blog.com/ielts-writing-samples/ielts-essays-band-8/ielts-essay-topic-computers-instead-of-teachers (adapted)

Task

In pairs, discuss the strengths of the piece of writing opposite. What are its weaknesses? How would you improve it?

Strengths	Development needs

Peer review

When you complete a draft of your own writing, you need to **review** it. This can be difficult. You've worked hard. You're fed up with the piece. You don't want to look at it again. You want to give it to the teacher/lecturer for a grade.

You **must** avoid this pitfall! Reviewing your work can make a huge difference to your grade, and remember that a teacher/lecturer **cannot correct your errors**. **You** must do this.

Self-correction

Decide on your strengths and weaknesses so that you can remove the latter and develop the former, ensuring that the whole piece improves.

Use your English department's self-correction code to check for technical errors.

Use the grade descriptors in Chapter 5.

Put the time and effort in to improving the work. This means a **word-by-word** and **line-by-line** check. More importantly, it means **taking action** when you do spot a problem. There is no substitute for this!

Task

Correct the errors in the following paragraph.

I was adviced by my teacher to check my work carefully there was no knead. my writing is always prefect and each and every sentence I right is always cheeked. I dont understand why mr grumble always picks on me i wood never except errors in my work

Spell checkers and grammar checkers

These **can** help, but be wary. Many spell checkers use American English, which has very different orthography from that of UK English. Equally, spell checkers cannot always read contexts. Few, if any, would spot that the following is wrong. Try this for yourself:

The teacher told me to practice my spelling.

Used as a noun, 'practice' is spelled correctly like this. Here, however, it is used as a verb so it takes the verbal form, 'practise'. It could be argued that this is both a spelling error and a grammatical error. It is also unlikely that a either a spell checker or a grammar checker would pick this up. You are welcome to try! Here's a spell checker you could use: www.jspell.com/public-spell-checker.html.

Sometimes, though, we find it very hard to see our own mistakes (see the diagram below). This is when the process of peer review can be very helpful. This is where a partner reviews your work **objectively** using the grade descriptors and technical accuracy criteria in Chapter 5. It is important here to accept that you will receive criticism. The idea is to be **constructive**, not **destructive**. That is the purpose of peer reviewing. This does not mean to put your work down; rather it means getting to know your work really well so that you can be offered advice to improve it. This cannot happen unless you both (reviewer and reviewee) know its strengths and weaknesses. One thing to bear in mind is that you too will be asked to review your partner's work!

Once you have completed the self and peer review process, you can then move on to **edit** your first draft in order to complete your **final draft**.

Can you spot the error?

CHAPTER FOUR

CREATIVE WRITING (PERSONAL/REFLECTIVE OR IMAGINATIVE)

PERSONAL

Personal writing can be either **real** or **imagined**, or a bit of both. Its aim is to describe how you **reacted** to a specific event. This will convey information about the experience to the reader and it will show your **feelings** about the event. In fact, **depth of feeling** is really important to this form of writing. So, you will **express** or even **explore** your own feelings and reactions in this kind of writing. To do this well, you need to describe your feelings as if they were very real and meaningful to you. This will show **self-awareness**. Often, this form of writing will also expose your own **personality** to the reader and show some insight into the experience. In other words, you are exploring your own feelings to reveal something new about the experience that you maybe didn't notice when it first happened.

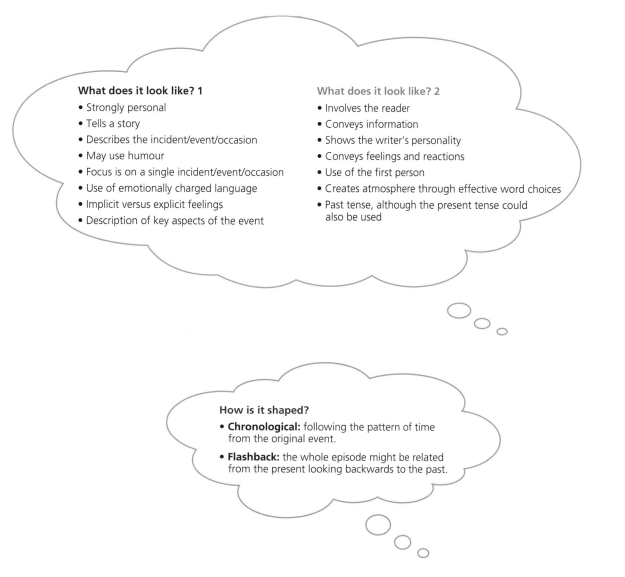

What does it look like? 1
- Strongly personal
- Tells a story
- Describes the incident/event/occasion
- May use humour
- Focus is on a single incident/event/occasion
- Use of emotionally charged language
- Implicit versus explicit feelings
- Description of key aspects of the event

What does it look like? 2
- Involves the reader
- Conveys information
- Shows the writer's personality
- Conveys feelings and reactions
- Use of the first person
- Creates atmosphere through effective word choices
- Past tense, although the present tense could also be used

How is it shaped?
- **Chronological:** following the pattern of time from the original event.
- **Flashback:** the whole episode might be related from the present looking backwards to the past.

Completed work

We are now going to **analyse the key stages** of a completed piece of work, bit by bit, to determine how is has been put together. We will examine a section from the **beginning**, the **middle** and the **end** of the writing.

Read this paragraph:

Holiday to Thailand

Beginning

I was seven years old and I had never been on an aeroplane before. When my dad asked me if I wanted to go to Thailand with him and his girlfriend, I immediately jumped at the chance and said yes! At the time the thoughts I was having could not compare to what Thailand was really like! I thought Thailand would be filled with villages and massive beaches with lots of palm trees, which it was, but it was far more beautiful and breathtaking!

Source: SQA Standard Grade Folio 2011

Analysis

- Reflection back to past.
- Implicit description through word choices: 'immediately jumped'.
- Use of punctuation to convey emotion: 'yes!'
- Comparison between the experience then (in the past) and how it is viewed now (in the present).
- Descriptive language: 'beautiful … breathtaking', also conveys emotion.

Now read on …

Middle

After we settled in, we had a look through the village and visited a Buddhist temple. The entire village was extremely different to anything I had experienced before and the people there did not have nearly as much of the high technology and riches as we have in Scotland. There were no supermarkets – just little shops. There were very few tarmac roads and most of the streets were made from sand and mud. I remember having great fun with the neighbours' children, playing football with them. I feel I experienced a simpler life to the life we have in Scotland and it really made me appreciate all the amenities that we have.

Task

Identify the techniques used in this paragraph and their effects.

Technique	Quotation	Effects
Reflection		
Narrative		
Comparison		
Explicit emotions		

Ending

We next travelled to an island off the coast of Thailand called Koh Samui. The journey was short and we travelled there in a small plane. We met up with my uncle and cousins who were also on holiday there. Koh Samui was absolutely amazing, with a beach I could only have dreamed about and situated only a five minute walk from the hotel where we were staying. The beach was extremely tropical with palm trees everywhere. I remember going snorkelling with my cousins and we saw the most wonderful fish and plant life. Our hotel had a swimming pool that never closed and my cousins and I had great fun there at night when no one was around. I had a fantastic time in Koh Samui and it was most definitely the highlight of my holiday.

Task

Identify the techniques used in this paragraph and their effects.

Technique	Quotation	Effects
Explicit emotions	I had a fantastic time	
Implicit emotions	we saw the most wonderful fish	Writer is awe-struck by the sealife
Narration		
Description		

Completed work

We will again **analyse the key stages** of another completed piece of work. This will give you practice in drawing out some key techniques in personal writing.

Read this section:

Recording King

Beginning

Ever since I was five years old, I have had a keen interest in the music industry and the lifestyle that follows it. I had grown up surrounded by a family in which music played a great role in day-to-day life. Both of my elder brothers played guitar with each other while I would sit in the corner fantasising about how one day maybe I could also learn to play this instrument. When I reached the age of nine I picked up a guitar for the first time. From then on I was hooked.

Source: SQA Intermediate 2 Writing Folio 2012

Task

Identify the techniques used in this paragraph and their effects.

Technique	Quotation	Effects
Narration		
Emotive word choice		

Middle

In November 2009 I was browsing the Internet looking at a number of guitars, to savour the beauty that each model held. There were guitars in all shapes and sizes, with price tags that matched their variety. As my eyes scanned the page a notice in small blue writing in the left-hand corner read, 'Recording King'. I double-clicked the small text to find the greatest instrument I had ever seen in my entire life. The stringed god was made of pure silver that reflected the light on to the floor in front of it. Its neck was oak and stretched up into the sky where the sharp headboard stuck out. I had to have it.

Task

Identify the techniques used in this paragraph and their effects.

Technique	Quotation	Effects
Narration		
Description		
Explicit emotions		

Ending

After a long time spent trying to convince my father, and a lot of money saving, I stood in the shop doorway hoping I would see this mythical guitar. I searched high and low, eyes darting around the room attempting to catch a glimpse of my quarry. I then took three steps into the second room. There it stood: the 'Recording King'.

It was more gorgeous than I had ever imagined. Perched up inside its glass case there was a sign that read, 'Do not touch.' At that moment my eyes drifted slowly down towards the three-digit price tag hanging from its flawless body: £560. In those seconds my dreams shattered. I would never be able to touch the guitar of my dreams. It was over. I turned my back to the shimmering beauty and began to trudge back towards the exit of the shop until a large hand fell gently on my shoulder. On the spot stood my dad, staring at me with pride. 'How about half each?' he asked.

'Thank you,' I whispered.

Task

Identify and fill in the techniques used in this paragraph and their effects.

Technique	Quotation	Effects

Website

- http://thenewmanexperience.wiki.lovett.org/Personal+Essay+Examples

REFLECTIVE

Reflective writing can be very similar to personal writing. It, too, concerns itself, usually, with a single idea, insight or experience and will include some **reflection on knowledge, thoughts or feelings** created by it. The most successful pieces of reflective writing, though, will normally involve an **exploration** of the topic/event, **but from a distance**. The writer is usually separated from the original event either by distance or time or because s/he has had a chance to think about it again so that s/he now sees it in a new light. The **tone** adopted in this kind of writing is usually thoughtful and, like all personal writing, it will convey a sense of the writer's personality as well as revealing their thought processes.

What does it look like?	
Strongly personal	Focus is on a single incident/event/occasion
Involves the reader	Use of the first person
Tells a story	Use of emotionally charged language
Conveys information	Creation of atmosphere through effective word choices
Describes the incident/event/occasion	Use of implicit versus explicit feelings
Shows the writer's personality	Use of the past tense, although the present tense could also be used
May use humour	Description of key aspects of the event is important
Focuses on conveying feelings and reactions	

How is it shaped?
Chronological: following the pattern of time from the original event.
Flashback: the whole episode might be related from the present looking backwards to the past. In this way, the writer can take advantage of the distance from the original event given by the separation of time.

Completed work

We will now analyse another completed piece of work. Again, the aim is to give you practice in drawing out some important techniques in reflective writing from key stages of the writing. In this case, a number of examples are selected from the middle of the writing as it is a fairly long piece.

Brotherly and sisterly love

Beginning

I could smell fear. I was scared and he was scared. The sharp seawater was clashing against my face as I forced myself under to push my brother to the surface before he ran out of air. That's all I was thinking about, making sure he was safe. I could taste the acidic salt water drying out the back of my throat, the nip of the salt attacking my taste buds, numbing my tongue. I could feel the seawater fighting against me. As I raised my head I could hear Jim breathing. It sounded like a panic attack.

Source: SQA Intermediate 2 Writing Folio 2012 (adapted)

This is an effective opening to a piece of reflective writing and it has a number of markers of the form:

- Use of the past tense.
- Use of long and short sentences.
- Use of the first person.
- Explicit description of feelings: 'I could smell fear.'
- Implicit description of feelings: 'I forced myself under.' Suggests a growing need for immediate action.
- Use of all of the senses: hearing, touch, smell, taste and sight.

Middle

I could feel nausea rising to the back of my throat and my nerves started to create painful knots in my stomach. My heart began to strangle itself as my breathing grew more laboured. I felt like I was dying. My blood went cold as I heard my brother fighting for his life while my body began to seize up as the dark, dark blue water pulled at me. I panicked.

Questions

Work in pairs to answer the following questions:

1. Some words are used to create the impression of things tightening around the writer. Quote three examples and say how effective you think they are.
2. The writer uses a technique here where long and short sentences are balanced. How many times does she do this? What is the effect?

Narrative modes

Writers can tell their tales in a number of different ways:

- First person narration: '**I** felt. **I** ran. **I** judged.'

- Second person narration: '**You** need to listen. **You** should not think badly.'

- Third person narration: '**He** told Jim it was the wrong decision.'

Think about the advantages of first person narration. We shall return to it at the end of this piece.

Middle

Before, I could see the temptation on his face. **He wanted** to jump. **He wanted** to prove everyone wrong. **He could swim** in deep waters and no one would stop him. **He wanted** to be like the big kids and swim freely although he was still young and learning. My dad was still at home. He trusted me with him. He trusted me with my brother's life. But before I could stop, he had already trusted himself and had gone for the leap. I panicked again.

Here, the technique of repetition is used in relation to the young brother and the dad. What are the effects?

Middle

I remember those days when we used to fight like there was no love between us. It felt like we weren't family. I didn't like those words. I got them almost every day, those dreaded words, 'I HATE YOU!'; not coming from the heart, but still making me think that I couldn't live with the thought that my brother hated me. Would he ever forgive me? I can't imagine life without this boy. He was and always will be a big part of my life. He means everything to me and that's why these words struck me, took away my smile and made me blank. That's why my heart crumbled when these little words were screamed into my face. And that's why my world stopped.

We can see here the writer exploring the relationship she has with her brother through the technique of **flashback**. We have moved from present to past, to a time when the brother and sister fought bitterly. The writer then goes on to imagine her **reactions** to this event.

Questions

1. What are her feelings?
2. What does the event reveal to her about her relationship with her brother?

Middle

After a breathtaking wrestle with the sea, I found myself and my brother safe, side by side on the pebble shore of the local beach. Both of us panting, shaking, petrified. The last two minutes had changed my life. We both turned and shared a brief smile. It was possibly the best second of my life. The only thing that mattered was that my brother was safe. After the sea tried to take my brother's life, the only thing that matters now is that I protect him forever. When I look back, this is the day I knew with absolute certainty that I loved my brother deeply. And that he loved me.

Tracking reflection

The reflection here is quite intense. Try now to **track the stages** of the reflection in the extract above. It has been started for you.

Safe, but cold and exhausted …

1
2
3

Ending

I gave him a hug as he looked up to me and he mouthed the words, 'I love you.' Those soft words made tears and created the warmest feeling in my stomach. It's like you just know that everything is going to be all right. Those wonderful words will always stay in my heart. Then he felt the cold of the water between his toes and backed away. I could see in his eyes that he was afraid, so I took his hand and we headed home.

It's changed the way I feel about 'brotherly and sisterly love'. Knowing that it gives you the strength and nerve to save them when they are in trouble makes you feel like you would do anything for your loved ones, and even if they do annoy you sometimes it does not mean that you don't love them. Now, when I see little children fighting, I can't help but think that they might one day develop the special bond we have, my brother and I.

Now, whenever I see my brother smile, it reminds me of that moment, a smile that reminds me of life. I now realise the reason he could have drowned was because he panicked. He knew how dangerous the sea was before he swam out too far for his little legs to touch the seabed. As soon as that toe lifted off the ground, he didn't know what to do. It was the first time he had challenged himself to swim in the open water.

➜

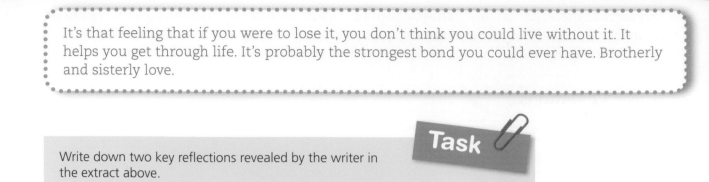

It's that feeling that if you were to lose it, you don't think you could live without it. It helps you get through life. It's probably the strongest bond you could ever have. Brotherly and sisterly love.

Task

Write down two key reflections revealed by the writer in the extract above.

Personal writing and the first person

As we noted earlier, writers can tell their tales in a number of different ways:

- First person narration: I …

- Second person narration: You …

- Third person narration: He/She/It …

You were asked to think about first person narration and its advantages to telling a tale. In personal writing, the use of the first person is vital as you are being asked to convey your feelings about an event and to pass on your reactions to that event. It is only possible to do this in a genuine and authentic way if you write personally, and to do that you need to use the first person. This also allows you to reveal your innermost thought to the reader and to 'wear your heart on your sleeve'.

We will look at the advantages of the other narrative modes later in the short-story section.

Possible personal/reflective topics

- I couldn't live without …
- My first love …
- My … means more to me than anything …
- An experience that changed my life …
- I remember when …
- My special place …
- A landmark moment for me was …
- A perfect friendship was formed when I …
- I was most influenced by …
- It all went wrong for me when …
- When I flew for the first time …
- When I took part in a dangerous sport/activity for the first time …
- The Museum of My Life. Write your own autobiography in which you display the milestones in your life so far.

Openers

- That was it. Dad's redundancy letter was there in front of me. I had no option. We had to move …
- The phone seemed to be screaming at me. Finally, I answered …
- From the prow of the ship, I gazed out over the clear, blue waters. My long anticipated journey had begun …
- A crackling fire. A great book. A purring cat. Bliss. I remember when …

Task

Choose **ONE** of the topics or openers from the opposite page or one you have found from a web search.

Write a piece of personal writing using some of the techniques explored in this section.

IMAGINATIVE

This can take a very wide range of forms, such as prose fiction (a short story, an episode from a novel, a drama script – scene, monologue, sketch), poetry, a television drama or soap script, a newspaper article, an advertisement, the opening sequence of a novel, a scene from a play, the script for a radio play, an extract from a biography, a letter (email format), a memoir, an essay, a pressure-group leaflet, the script of a speech (educational, political), a piece of description or a series of linked or contrasting descriptive pieces.

Short story

Genre features	Some broad ideas: short stories could be based on the following
Use of setting in time and place.	A person, a place, an object.
Description of setting through appropriate word choices.	An event, a situation, a relationship.
Use of realistic/believable details to support setting.	An argument, a conflict, a misunderstanding.
Establishing an atmosphere/mood appropriate to the form of story being written.	A discovery, a choice, a dilemma.
Creation of setting appropriate to purpose/genre. If a horror story, then unease, trepidation and even fear might be the desired intention.	A prejudice, a delusion, an obsession.
The creation of characters through physical description, through interaction with other characters, and through revelation of their thoughts, actions and speech (dialogue).	A memory, an image, an insight.
Punctuation of direct speech.	An experience, an issue, an activity.
Hints that all might not be well.	
Suggestion of a crisis to follow (or in the past).	
Development of a theme.	
Creation of a controlled plot.	

How are they shaped?

Broadly, short stories can be structured like this:

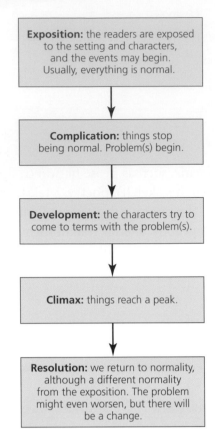

Narrative mode

Point of view is the perspective from which a story is told by its **narrator**. This might be in the **first person** where the story is told from the **viewpoint** of a **speaker** who is also involved in the action in the story. We recognise this from the use of the pronoun 'I'. Remember, too, that this fact might cloud her/his judgement about events!

Alternatively, the **writer** might tell the story, impersonally, in the **third person**. In this way, the writer gains certain advantages. S/he can expose the thoughts of all of the characters. We recognise the use of the **third person** when we see the pronouns 'he/she/it' being used.

Occasionally, writers might also make use of the **second person** form of address by using the pronoun 'you'. The intention here is usually to identify closely with the reader(s) in order to establish a strong rapport with them.

Completed work

We will now analyse a completed piece of work using **exposition**, **complication**, **development**, **climax** and **resolution**. The aim is to give you practice in drawing out some techniques vital to the creation of effective short stories.

Here I am

Exposition (and complication)

So here I am, kneeling by you, your faceless gravestone staring back at me, the rain beating off my face like bullets from a gun, thinking to myself that it should be me lying here, not you. It's been ten years since you left and not a day passes when I don't think about what happened. The detailed images fill my head day and night. There have been those times when I see someone in the street and beg someone, anyone, that it's you, but when I take a second glance I know it can never be. It's moments like these when I find myself talking to you, knowing that I will never get an answer. This sends my mind into overload flashing back to that eventful day all those years ago, the images becoming more detailed every time.

Source: SQA Intermediate 2 Writing Folio 2012 (adapted)

Questions

1. What is the setting? How do we know?
2. What do we know of the central character?
3. What narrative mode is being used? Why?
4. How would you describe the atmosphere?
5. What is likely to happen next? (What do we need to know to allow the story to develop?)

Development told through flashback

Do you remember? We were sat there at my desk drinking our third coffee of the day, having one of those awkward small talk conversations when that sound, that ear piercing sound shuddered through the entire office as a huge plane destroyed what used to be the top few floors of our offices. Bits of flaming debris began to catapult to the floor and many survivors from the floors above decided to take that suicidal plunge to the ground, knowing that it would be the last thing they would ever do. It was either that or be burned alive. No luck. Then there was you and me. Being slightly more fortunate, we were a few floors below and could set our sights on escaping this apocalypse.

Questions

1. Flashback is where the narration shifts from present to past. How does the flashback complicate or add to what we already know?
2. The sound of the collision is made clear by the writer. How is this done?
3. How could the description(s) be improved?

Climax

We ran frantically towards the stairway, elbows and fists blocking our paths as others clambered in the same direction. Just then a loud thud came echoing from above and the roofs from floors above came crashing down on us. Trapped. Unable to feel my legs, sandwiched between two huge sections of roof and tons of rubble, I looked over to you through the haze of debris. I shouted your name. No answer. I panicked. I shouted louder. You replied, a faint whisper, but it was enough for me to know you were still here. Stuck even worse than me, huge rocks laid like a thick carpet over your fragile body with only your head to be seen. A tear trickled down my face at the sight, but I spoke to you, kept you talking, breathing, anything to make sure you were still alive and with me.

I gave up, after I felt the minutes turn to hours. We were two needles in a haystack. I knew there were people above us; each footstep would send dust clouds whirling around me, but still they could not hear my cries for help. A light came flashing down on me. You were gone.

Questions

1. The situation is becoming clearer now. What has happened?
2. What is likely to happen next?
3. How do we know this?

Sentence variety

Your writing will be far more interesting for your reader if you vary the sentences you use. Too much of the same thing gets boring pretty quickly! There are a number of **sentence types**.

- **Long sentences** make complex points or describe things in detail or stress the length of time something takes, for example:

We ran frantically towards the stairway, elbows and fists blocking our paths as others clambered in the same direction.

- **Short sentences** capture the reader's attention and create impact because they stand out against longer sentences:

- **Simple sentences** have a **subject** and a **verb**.

  Statements state facts/make assertions:

I   panicked.

- **Minor sentences** don't have main verbs in them, although their meaning is still very clear. This example is plainly short for, 'I/We   was/were   trapped':

Trapped.

- **Compound sentences** join two complete sentences with the help of a co-ordinator. In the case below, 'and':

Just then a loud thud came echoing from above and the roofs from floors above came crashing down on us.

Co-ordinator

- **Complex sentences** have a **main clause** joined by one or more **subordinate clauses**. The subordinate clause in this sentence, 'I felt the minutes turn to hours', leaves the reader wondering, 'Why?' and requires the main clause, 'I gave up,' to complete the meaning:

After   I felt the minutes turn to hours,   I gave up.

Subordinate conjunction   Subordinate clause   Main clause

Other ways of varying sentences

- Sometimes **questions** are used to bring the reader deeper into the events, or even **rhetorical questions**, where a reply is obviously not intended, but where the intention, again, is to involve the reader more closely.
- **Repetition** allows the writer to emphasise key points.
- **Single sentence paragraphs** stand out and draw attention to the words, which can **contrast** with what has gone before.
- **Exclamations** convey sudden surprise or emotion.
- **Climax** is a technique used to build things up.
- **Anti-climax** is the opposite of this where, having built things up, the writer lowers the tension, possibly to contrast with the earlier points.
- **Lists** can be used for different purposes.
- **Parallel sentence structures with variation** can be used to garner evidence in favour of a point. Here the third person personal pronoun is followed by different verbs, but they all create one meaning, i.e. that he put a lot of effort into his studies:

He read. **He** worked. **He** thought.

- **Asyndetic lists** are lists without conjunctions. The omission of conjunctions creates the impression of speed or haste, of things being done without drawing breath:

She hopped, skipped, ran to the door.

- **Polysyndetic lists** are lists with conjunctions. These can be used for different purposes:

  - to suggest a build-up:

She walked then she ran then she cried.

  - to suggest equal importance:

He was tall and he was handsome and he was clever.

Try to vary the sentences in your own writing as the writer has done here.

Resolution

Back to the story now.

From that day until now, I still think about you day in day out. No cup of coffee has tasted the same since.

Questions

The narrative (story) now switches back, from the flashback, to the present.

1. There is no dialogue in the story. Would it have been improved with it?
2. We never learn the names of the two central characters. Would we have had more sympathy with them if we had?
3. How would you have improved this ending?

Possible narrative topics

Short-story titles:

- The Recluse
- Charmer
- The Wedding Ceremony
- Gap Year
- The Return
- The Bracelet
- Celebration
- Storm
- The Last Time
- A New Man
- Planetfall
- Little Black Dress
- The Right Path

Openers

- There he stood. Waiting. As if he had been there forever. Tate crossed the busy street ...
- It was an ordinary day. Just like any other, really. Except that Sal was watching her brother walking towards her and she hadn't seen him in ten years ...
- The door was jammed. He pushed harder this time. It opened. Syme couldn't believe his eyes ...
- She stared at the letter. Dare she open it? She reached for it ...
- There was a strange smell in the air. Odd. Disturbing even. He leapt from his bed ...

Task

Choose **EITHER** one of the titles or openers above **OR** an idea from the websites below and then write the short story.

Websites

- www.creative-writing-now.com/short-story-ideas.html
- www.daviddfriedman.com/Miscellaneous/story_ideas.htm

Poem or set of thematically linked poems

There is a variety of approaches and a great many forms you might use here, so it is unrealistic to prescribe exactly what a poem should look like. When writing poetry, you should bear in mind the following:

- word choices and the arrangement of words into lines and verses/stanzas

- the surprising connections poetry makes between words

- its often condensed use of language, where meaning is packed into few words

- its greater use of figurative language, such as metaphors and similes

- its use of sound (onomatopoeia and alliteration), rhythm or rhyme

- its unusual word order and arrangement of ideas and images.

A poem should also present its topic in a striking and original way. Whatever the range and variety of its references and detail, the theme of a poem should be focused and clear through its imagery. A poem should also contain a clear sense of the writer's involvement with the topic. This might be imaginative or emotional or intellectual, or all three combined.

Things to consider

As you can probably tell, writing poetry is not an easy task. As well as this, all poetry pieces will be marked as normal by SQA markers. Markers, however, might refer poetry scripts to the Team Leader or to the Principal Assessor, at which point grades may (or may not) be altered.

There are other considerations, too, as the rules applied to other pieces of writing do not apply to poetry. Length, for example, is judged by appropriacy as opposed to fulfilling the usual count of 1000 words. Here, markers are faced with the dilemma of judging whether a brief piece of poetry deserves as much as a longer short story. Equally, markers may be much more experienced and comfortable at grading other forms of writing. Finally, poetry pieces are rare; a marker might not mark even one in a whole allocation of marking. As such, there may be little or nothing else with which to compare it.

Advice

- Writing poetry is to be encouraged, but you might want to think twice before submitting it as part of your National 5 portfolio.

- Take the advice of your teacher. If you have been advised already that your work is of a high quality (perhaps you have won a poetry competition) then by all means submit it.

- Submit poetry only if you, yourself, read and appreciate poetry.

Still interested?

Glasgow Sonnet 1

Edwin Morgan

A mean wind wanders through the backcourt trash. (A)

Hackles on puddles rise, old mattresses (B)

puff briefly and subside. Play-fortresses (B)

of brick and bric-a-brac spill out some ash. (A)

Four storeys have no windows left to smash, (A)

but the fifth a chipped sill buttresses (B)

mother and daughter the last mistresses (B)

of that black block condemned to stand, not crash. (A)

Around them the cracks deepen, the rats crawl. (C)

The kettle whimpers on a crazy hob. (D)

Roses of mould grow from ceiling to wall. (C)

The man lies late since he has lost his job, (D)

smokes on one elbow, letting his coughs fall (C)

thinly into an air too poor to rob. (D)

Source: www.edwinmorgan.com/pop_carcanet_sonnet1.html

Let's look more closely.

- This poem has fourteen lines. This is the number in a **sonnet**. How are the lines arranged within those fourteen lines?
- This poem rhymes. It rhymes like this: ABBA ABBA CDC DCD.
- This means that the following lines rhyme: 1 and 4, 2 and 3, 5 and 8, 6 and 7. Then 9, 11 and 13, and 10, 12 and 14.

As you can see, this is a pretty complex arrangement!

Let's look at it again.

- There are **two parts** to this poem: the first eight lines have a particular rhyme scheme in common – ABBA. Then lines nine to fourteen have another rhyme scheme, CDC, which then inverts in the last triplet to DCD.
- How does it work? The **octet** deals with the environment outside the flats, while the **sestet** looks at what is happening within the building.
- So, we have two **stanzas** (quatrains) making up the first eight lines (known as an **octet**), and two shorter stanzas (triplets this time as they each have three lines), known as **sestets**. This is known as a **Petrarchan sonnet** structure. Petrarch was an Italian poet whose themes were based on his love for Laura, a woman who did not return his love, unfortunately. So, Morgan is using this to contrast with the modern urban setting of his poem.

Complete the chart below.

Technique	Example	Effect
Word choices and in the arrangement of words into lines and verses/stanzas		
The surprising connections poetry makes between words		
Its often-condensed use of language, where meaning is packed into few words		
Its greater use of figurative language, such as metaphors and similes		
Its use of sound (onomatopoeia and alliteration), rhythm or rhyme		
Its unusual word order and arrangement of ideas and images		

Here is another poem set in Glasgow.

Glasgow, 5 March 1971

Edwin Morgan

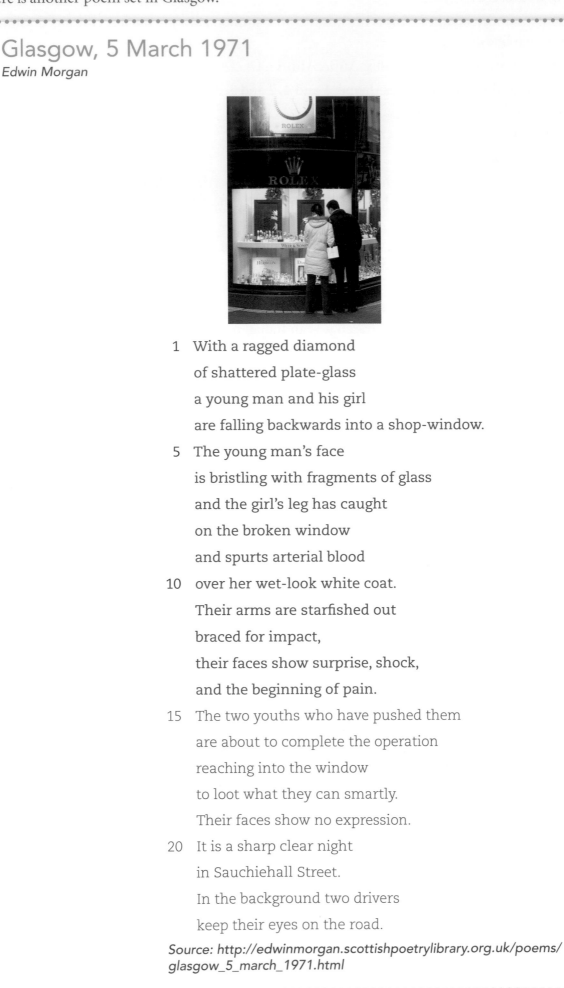

1   With a ragged diamond

of shattered plate-glass

a young man and his girl

are falling backwards into a shop-window.

5   The young man's face

is bristling with fragments of glass

and the girl's leg has caught

on the broken window

and spurts arterial blood

10   over her wet-look white coat.

Their arms are starfished out

braced for impact,

their faces show surprise, shock,

and the beginning of pain.

15   The two youths who have pushed them

are about to complete the operation

reaching into the window

to loot what they can smartly.

Their faces show no expression.

20   It is a sharp clear night

in Sauchiehall Street.

In the background two drivers

keep their eyes on the road.

Source: http://edwinmorgan.scottishpoetrylibrary.org.uk/poems/
glasgow_5_march_1971.html

This poem is organised very differently from the sonnet. Let's examine how. Like the sonnet, it has two parts:

- **Part 1** is from the opening line to 'pain.'
- **Part 2** is from 'The two youths' to 'road.'

Part 1 deals with an incident in Glasgow's Sauchiehall Street that happened in 1971. A young couple has been pushed through a jeweller's shop window. The first part of the poem describes their fall and the injuries they sustain.

Part 2 deals with **how** the incident happened. It was no accident.

This section has a number of movements:
- The young couple has been used by two young thieves to gain entry to the shop.
- The robbers have no feelings about the two victims.
- Visibility is good so it is unlikely the incident has been missed.
- The drivers 'keep' their eyes on the road.

Questions

1. What is going on in lines 1–4?
2. How would lines 1–4 be written as prose?
3. What is going on in lines 5–10?
4. What techniques are used in lines 5–10 to show the extent of the injuries?
5. What is going on in lines 11–14?
6. What effect is the poet trying to achieve in lines 11–14? How successful has he been?
7. In lines 15–18 we discover that the couple has been used by two young thieves to gain entry to the shop but the word 'operation' is unusual. Why is it used?
8. In line 19 we learn that the robbers have no feelings about the two victims. How is this idea conveyed?
9. In lines 20–21 we know that visibility is good so it is unlikely the incident has been missed. How does Morgan ensure that we are absolutely clear on this point?
10. In lines 22–23 the drivers 'keep' their eyes on the road. What does this tell us about their actions? What is the poet trying to make us think about in this poem?

Possible topics for poetry

- Some very short poetry forms, such as haikus, while interesting, might not be ideal as portfolio submissions as they could be deemed to be simply much too brief for the normal word count.
- To rhyme or not to rhyme? Remember that you will not necessarily gain marks for writing in rhyme as all of the other components of poetry have to be present, too.
- 'Free verse' or unrhymed poetry might appeal to some writers, but the pitfall here is that what you produce might read like flowery prose rather than poetry.
- Technically challenging forms such as the sonnet might be a way forward, but, again, you would really have to produce a series of thematically linked sonnets to move some way towards the word limit, and this would increase the challenge considerably.

Some possible titles

- Pandora's Box
- When I Was Young
- The Tender Trap
- The City at Night
- Twilight
- Not a Moment too Soon
- Revenge
- The Face

Dramatic script (scene, monologue, sketch)

If you choose to write a drama script for your portfolio, you should be able to demonstrate a range of specific skills that illustrate your understanding of the genre.

The **aim** of a drama script is to **entertain** and to **provoke thought** in the audience/readers.

In particular, you should be able to:

- **create characters** who are credible, interesting and capable of provoking a response in the reader
- make effective use of **dialogue** and show an awareness of script notes on non-verbal communication – tone, gesture, body language – as well as indicating stage directions, special effects and other production notes related to drama
- establish a **setting** in place and time
- develop a **central interest** or **theme**
- produce a particular **effect**, **mood** or **atmosphere**
- present a script in a **format** appropriate to its purpose – stage, television, radio
- **convince** the reader of the potential of the script for actual presentation in an appropriate medium, ensuring always that stage directions, technical effects and other production notes are directly linked to the action.

Possible topics for dramatic scripts

- an event, a situation, a relationship
- an argument, a conflict, a misunderstanding
- a discovery, a choice, a dilemma
- a prejudice, a delusion, an obsession
- a mood, a memory, a feeling
- an idea, an issue, an experience

You could produce a short **one-act play**, or create a **scene** from a whole play. Another option is to produce a **monologue**. This is where there is only one character or 'voice' speaking.

The SQA encourages the use of a wide range of different language forms and, in particular, Scottish language forms.

Remember that there are key characteristics you need to develop in any drama:

- **Setting:** time and place.
- **Characterisation:** what characters do and say.
- **Dialogue:** what is said, how it is said and to whom it is said.
- **Plot:** main events or character interactions.
- **Structure:** exposition, conflict, resolution/climax.

Plays often open with an **exposition**, to establish the main **characters**, their relationships and their world. Later, the main character (**protagonist**) is confronted with a problem (**conflict**). Her/his attempts to deal with this lead to a second and more dramatic situation, known as the **turning point**. The **plot** then deals with the protagonist's attempts to resolve the problem, but this usually creates more problems. Part of the reason the protagonist seems unable to resolve the problem(s) is that they do not yet have the skills or character traits to do so. When they do develop these it is referred to as **character development**. Finally, the end of the play, featuring the **resolution** of the story and the **climax**, is when the main tensions are brought to **resolution**.

Stage directions

- Instructions for stage setting are written on the left of the page.
- The name of the speaker is written on the left of the page.
- Extra instructions for the actor are written in brackets.
- Every time the setting of the play changes, a new scene is started.
- At the start of each new scene, the setting is described.

Elements of drama

In The Poetics, Aristotle outlined the key elements of drama in his analysis of the Sophoclean tragedy Oedipus Rex. Particularly significant to the modern audience are: Thought, Theme, Ideas, Action or Plot, Characters, Language.

Theme

What the play means (theme) as opposed to what happens in it (plot). Sometimes the theme is clearly stated in the title. Alternatively, it may be stated through dialogue by a character acting as the playwright's voice. Or it may be that the theme is less obvious and emerges only after some study or thought about issues that emerge from the plot or characters.

Plot

What happens in the play; the story as opposed to the theme. The plot must have a structure so that each action starts the next rather than being disconnected. In the plot of a play, characters are involved in conflict that has a pattern of movement. The action and movement in the play begins from the initial conflict, through action, to turning point, to climax, and finally resolution.

Characters

These are the people who carry out the actions. In ancient times, each character had a distinct personality, age, appearance, set of beliefs and socio-economic background, and spoke in a particular way.

Language

The word choices made by the writer and the way the actors choose to speak those words. This moves the plot and action along.

This is an extract from the opening scene of *Macbeth*, by William Shakespeare:

SCENE I. A desert place.

Thunder and lightning. Enter three Witches.

First Witch

When shall we three meet again?

In thunder, lightning, or in rain?

Second Witch

When the hurlyburly's done,

When the battle's lost and won.

Third Witch

That will be ere the set of sun.

Questions

1. The words 'desert[ed]' together with 'thunder and lightning' create a very particular setting. Describe it.
2. The stage directions are short, but effective. 'Enter three Witches.' What does this tell us about the likely theme of the play?
3. The Third Witch says little, but shows an unusual ability. What is that ability?
4. Macbeth himself is absent from this scene, which creates setting, highlights themes to be developed and points to action(s) yet to happen – a battle. Why might the central character wish to meet with these witches?

Ideas for drama scripts

- A monologue by a train driver.
- A nightmarish job interview.
- Two men narrowly avoid a major traffic accident.
- A monologue by a night worker.
- A relationship beginning to turn sour.
- Meeting an old friend after years of separation.
- The last meeting before a friend leaves for university.

Task

Choose **ONE** of the topics above and then write an opening scene.

DESCRIPTIVE

The key aim of descriptive writing is to describe a person, place or thing vividly and in such a way that the reader can visualise the topic and feel like they are part of the experience. In this kind of writing, the writer can express his or her feelings on a subject.

Another important aim is to capture the readers' attention. This involves being aware of the audience's preferences and being able to use language to maintain their interest.

What are its features?

Descriptive writing is characterised by elaborate use of sensory details, such as how things look, sound, feel, taste or smell.

'Experience' the description

- The idea here is to bring your reader into the world you have described by making it easy for them to visualise it, for example letting them experience an awful smell at first hand:

The fetid stench of liquefying cabbage.

- It may also use figurative language, for example words, phrases, symbols and ideas – such as simile, hyperbole, metaphor, symbolism, personification – in such a way as to evoke mental images and sense impressions. These details will enable the reader to picture or relive what the writer is describing.
- Effective descriptive writing will **show**, but not **tell**.

The 'tell' sentence:

- will show what is going on explicitly:

It was dark.

The 'show' sentence:

- makes the readers think and involves them more in the description, for example:

Inky blackness crept across the scarred landscape obscuring all light.

- will use vivid and precise adjectives, adverbs and powerful verbs when describing the topic, but these will not be overused
- will make effective use of the connotative meanings of words – their emotional charges
- will usually vary sentence length and word order to engage the reader.

How is it shaped?

Descriptive writing generally includes an introduction, the main body of the text and then a conclusion centred on a chosen theme. The writing style is expressive and may include descriptions, opinions, comparisons, personal perceptions and sensory perceptions. Good descriptive writing is always organised. This might be done:

- chronologically (in time)
- spatially (by location)
- in order of importance
- or when describing a person, you might begin with a physical description, followed by how that person thinks, feels and acts.

A work in progress

We will now analyse a completed piece of work. The aim is to give you practice in working with some of the techniques vital to the creation of effective descriptive writing.

The Persistence of Memory

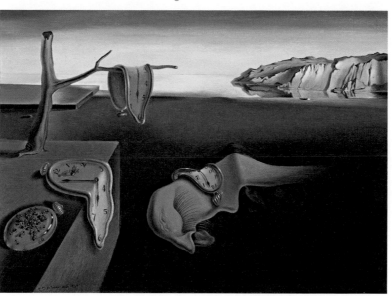

There hardly ever was a single artist who understood the meaning of the phrase 'time flies' as well as Dali did. Making people actually see the way time passes, Dali created the most memorable surrealist artwork ever, The Persistence of Memory.

Apart from the soft clocks, the most unusual detail of the picture is the palette. Using a mixture of yellow, blue, brick-red and brown, the artist succeeds in conveying, through his picture, a very specific mood.

The objects in the picture look both unbelievable and attractive, yet it is hard to focus on a single element. It feels like the artist offers a puzzle that is hard even to define, let alone to solve.

I believe that this is the most mysterious journey into the mind of a genius. This picture makes me feel awe and surprise at the same time. The picture reminds one somewhat of the riddles from childhood, which one could never solve.

However, most people consider this picture a sign that the artist entered another stage of his development – the scientific stage.

Anyway, one of the most mysterious artworks ever created, The Persistence of Memory will make a large number of future generations still gasp in awe at the genius of Dali.

Source: http://overnightessay.com/blog/2012/04/26/a-descriptive-essay-example-learn-what-makes-a-perfect-writing (adapted)

Task

Work with a partner to consider the following:

1. What is the subject?
2. How is this an example of 'showing', not 'telling'?
3. The techniques used to capture the readers' attention.
4. The use of the sense of sight.

A work in progress

Another chance to practise your skills!

A walk in the park

Everyone needs to take a break from the crazy pace of the New York City lifestyle, once in a while. When I ask myself where the best place to do that is, I do not have to think for more than a second. My favourite spot in NYC is the Van Cortlandt Park, with its long paving trails that I so much like to ride on my bike, passing jungles of trees and bushes so wild that they make you believe you have escaped the city completely, and are somewhere in the middle of a real, rich forest. I love its ample, spacious green valleys that remind me of those gorgeous Scottish hills you can sometimes see in the movies, with white, puffy dots of sheep, and lonely, chunky trees, here and there. I love the impetuous dashing stream of the Tibbets Brook, and the contrasting calm, and breathless pacifying waters, of the Van Cortlandt lake.

Last week I made my annual escape to the park. I was alone, didn't take my bike this time, only my camera and my five senses, which was all I needed to enjoy a day away from work, buzz and crowds. I first went to the Parade Ground, watched as a couple of cricket players ran back and forth in their crisp white mantles that sparkled in the sun like diamonds. Just like those sheep in the Scottish hills, only whiter and much faster. Not wanting to get burned in the bright morning sun rays, I quickly moved on to reach my destination – the meadow grass plot in the middle of the oak forest. I had spotted this location before, and promised myself I would go there again.

As I moved through the dense forest of the park, I pushed away the ample fluffy branches that came in my way, trying not to hurt any of the big flat leaves or neat, perfect acorns that covered each branch. Wanting to be closer to nature, I decided not to take the pathway but, instead, to go directly through the forest. It was as if there wasn't a sign of civilization around me at all. The oak trees were my favourite, with their wide, strong, mossy trunks and tender, roundish leaves. The air was still wet from the early morning shower. While everywhere, in the open, it had already been very dry and hot, as if there hadn't been a shower at all; the shadows of the forest still preserved the moist humidity, intensified by the smell of wet moss and last year's leaves that still lay on the ground. I loved this deep moist air, saturated with oxygen and filled with freshness.

Source: http://academichelp.net/samples/essays/descriptive/walk-in-the-park.html (adapted)

Task

Work in pairs to complete these charts:

Paragraph 1

Technique	Quotation	Effects
The effective use of adjectives	'Long paving trails'	
Metaphor	'Jungles of trees' 'Puffy dots of sheep'	
Personification	'Impetuous dashing stream' 'Calm … breathless pacifying waters'	

Paragraph 2

Technique	Quotation	Effects
Onomatopoeia	'Buzz'	
Simile	'Sparkled in the sun like diamonds'	
Alliteration	'Burned in the bright morning sun rays'	

Paragraph 3

Technique	Quotation	Effects
Contrast	'The air was still wet … very dry and hot'	
Precise verbs	'Saturated' 'Loved'	
Precise adjectives	'<u>Perfect</u> acorns' '<u>Wide</u>, <u>strong</u>, <u>mossy</u> trunks'	

Descriptive writing ideas

- Ice. Endless blue ice for a hundred miles in every direction. Sharp, cold, beautiful.
- Gold. Endless golden fields stretching and swaying in gentle winds to the far horizons.
- On the tall peaks the glistening sunbeams play,
  With a light heart our course we may renew,
  The first whose footsteps print the mountain dew.
- In flakes of light upon the mountainside;
  Where with loud voice the power of water shakes
  The leafy wood, or sleeps in quiet lakes.
- A silent city street. Sleek cars glisten. Frost dusts the pavement.
- A panorama of blue. Deep, ocean blue. Until the sea meets the far horizon.
- Inside. Looking out. Small room. Cocooned. Warm. Safe.
- Outside. Looking in. Blue-black eternities around me. Stars. Cold. Scared.

Websites

You might find these helpful. Try Google for more!

- www2.actden.com/writ_den/tips/paragrap/describe.htm
- www.thewritingsite.org
- http://teacher.scholastic.com/writewit/diary/index.htm
- www.webenglishteacher.com/descriptive.html

Task

Choose **EITHER** one of the titles **OR** an idea from one of the websites above, and then produce a piece of descriptive writing.

CHAPTER FIVE

ASSESSMENT: SAMPLE WRITING PIECES GRADED

Remember that your portfolio should be made up of **two** pieces of writing; one broadly creative and one broadly discursive.

How will these be graded?

Technical accuracy may be determined before using the descriptors. SQA says that, 'satisfactory technical accuracy is a requirement for a mark of 8 or above.' Technical accuracy does not mean writing that is without errors. It does mean that these errors will not be significant, namely that they will not impede meaning. **Paragraphing**, **sentence construction**, **spelling** and **punctuation**, the key technical features, will be sufficiently accurate (for National 5) so that meaning is clear at first reading.

So, you should consider the way in which you create sentences. It is about word choices and word order. Are there too many adjectives or too few? Are there too many adverbs or not enough? Have you chosen the right words to create the effects you are trying to achieve? Finally, is what you are trying to communicate clear, at first reading? If not, you need to review what you have written. More importantly, you need to make changes.

> # Remember!
>
> **Technical accuracy** does not mean error-free work, but rather work in which the errors are not significant. **This is a requirement for a pass grade**.
>
> The key features are: **paragraphing**, **sentence construction**, **spelling** and **punctuation**.

Broad descriptors

Category	Description
15–13	Very good (for the level).
12–10	Good.
9–7	Satisfactory. **N.B. See below**
6–4	Approaching satisfactory.
3–1	Significant flaws.

Assessing the writing

Let's take a closer look.

The first thing to note is that there are (broadly) three pass categories:

- 15–13
- 12–10
- 9–7. Note that a mark of 7 is a fail.

There are two grade descriptors: one for creative and one for discursive writing. Each of these has two categories: content and style.

	15–13	12–10	9–7	6–4	3–1
Discursive content	• Attention to purpose and audience is consistent. • Information shows evidence of careful research, is presented to maximise impact, and is sequenced to highlight key points. • Ideas/techniques deployed to inform/argue/discuss/persuade have a very good degree of objectivity/depth/insight/persuasive force and are used to convey a clear line of thought/appropriate stance/point of view.	• Attention to purpose and audience is consistent, in the main. • Information shows evidence of relevant research and is presented in a clear sequence. • Ideas/techniques deployed to inform/argue/discuss/persuade have a good degree of objectivity/depth/insight/persuasive force and are used to convey a clear line of thought/stance/point of view.	• Attention to purpose and audience is reasonably well sustained. • Information shows evidence of some research and is presented in a clear sequence. • Ideas/techniques used to inform/argue/discuss/persuade convey a line of thought/stance/point of view.	• Attention to purpose and audience is not always sustained. • Information shows a little relevant research, but is not always presented in a manner that enhances meaning. • Ideas/techniques used to inform/argue/discuss/persuade are not always convincing and the line of thought is not consistently clear. The stance may tend towards the personal or anecdotal.	Writing pieces in this category are likely to be very rare and would be characterised by one or more of the following. • Weak attention to purpose and audience. • Very thin content. • No attempt at using language effectively. • Significant errors in sentence construction/ paragraphing/spelling. • Brevity of response. • Irrelevance. 0 marks will be awarded where the candidate shows no understanding of the task, and displays none of the skills of writing in different genres or for different audiences and purposes.
Discursive style	• The features of the chosen genre are deployed effectively. • Word choice is varied and often used to create particular effects. • The structure of the piece enhances the purpose/meaning.	• The features of the chosen genre are deployed, mostly successfully. • Word choice is apposite and used, at times, to create an effect. • The structure of the piece supports the purpose/meaning.	• The features of the chosen genre are deployed with a degree of success. • Word choice is effective, in the main. • The structure of the piece is appropriate to the purpose/meaning.	• There is an attempt to deploy the features of the chosen genre. • Word choice lacks variety. • The structure of the piece is not appropriate to purpose/meaning.	

	15–13	12–10	9–7	6–4	3–1
Creative content	• Attention to purpose and audience is consistent. As appropriate to genre: • The piece displays very good creativity. • Feelings/reactions/experiences are expressed/explored with a very good degree of self-awareness/involvement/insight/sensitivity.	• Attention to purpose and audience is consistent, in the main. As appropriate to genre: • The piece displays good creativity. • Feelings/reactions/experiences are expressed/explored with a good degree of self-awareness/involvement/insight/sensitivity.	• Attention to purpose and audience is reasonably well sustained. As appropriate to genre: • The piece shows some creativity. • Feelings/reactions/experiences are expressed/explored with a sense of involvement.	• Attention to purpose and audience is not always sustained. As appropriate to genre: • The piece has little evidence of creativity. • Experiences are expressed, but not always convincingly.	Writing pieces in this category are likely to be very rare and would be characterised by one or more of the following. • Weak attention to purpose and audience. • Very thin content. • No attempt at using language effectively. • Significant errors in sentence construction/paragraphing/spelling. • Brevity of response. • Irrelevance. 0 marks will be awarded where the candidate shows no understanding of the task, and displays none of the skills of writing in different genres or for different audiences and purposes.
Creative style	• The features of the chosen genre are deployed effectively. • Word choice is varied and often used to create particular effects. • The structure of the piece enhances the purpose/meaning.	• The features of the chosen genre are deployed, mostly successfully. • Word choice is apposite and used, at times, to create an effect. • The structure of the piece supports the purpose/meaning.	• The features of the chosen genre are deployed with a degree of success. • Word choice is effective, in the main. • The structure of the piece is appropriate to the purpose/meaning.	• There is an attempt to deploy the features of the chosen genre. • Word choice lacks variety. • The structure of the piece is not appropriate to purpose/meaning.	

Creative	
Content	**Features**
Relevance	(purpose) is all about staying on task. To this end, it is worth reviewing this at the end of each paragraph you write. Remember! *Every* paragraph.
Creativity	could refer to any component of the writing. It refers to the extent to which the writer has been imaginative in the way in which the writing has been constructed, for example: • Closely involving the audience through the use of the second person. • The use of a structure that is unusual. • The use of a surprise ending. • The deployment of unusual or highly effective punctuation. • Sentencing that creates particular effects. • The unexpected rendering of emotions or feelings or reactions. • Density of reflection. The list is endless as there are so many ways to do something just a little different in your piece of writing. Most importantly, creativity shows your ability to create a piece of writing independently once you have explored models in class.
Feelings/reactions	refers to the extent to which personal/reflective pieces demonstrate self-awareness/involvement in the experience described and sensitivity towards the topic.
Style	**Features**
Genre	refers to the extent to which you have successfully used the key features of the genre in which you have chosen to write.
Word choice	refers to how appropriate and varied your word choices are.
Structure	concerns how your writing is shaped. It is not just about paragraphing: • Does it have an overall shape? For example, does it have a clear beginning, middle and conclusion? • Is it paragraphed? Is the paragraphing accurate? Does the paragraphing highlight what is most important in the writing?

Discursive	
Content	**Features**
Research	for informative or report writing has been conducted carefully and has been recast and presented in such a way that key points are highlighted.
Style	**Features**
Ideas/techniques	used to persuade are of quality, have depth and convey a clear line of thought or point of view. Length restrictions are very clearly stated for the portfolio. One thousand words is the upper limit.

Applying the grade descriptors

Knowing how your work will be assessed is very important. This gives you an in-depth knowledge of how the grade descriptors will be applied to your own work, which will help you to improve it. One way of doing this is to apply the descriptors to writing pieces. The following samples are all available on the SQA's website: www.sqa.org.uk. Expert commentaries have also been written to give you a good idea of the grades that might be applied to these pieces of writing by the SQA.

Hint!

Markers will grade your work **holistically**. This means they will consider all aspects of it when making a judgement about the grade; not just its spelling or sentence construction, for example. They are asked to look for its strengths and advised that giving a piece of writing 15/15 does not mean that it is a perfect piece of work.

You will notice that each category has a range of marks. For example, the highest category has a range of 15–13. For the writing pieces below, decide which category most closely describes the piece of writing.

- Where the writing almost matches the level above, the highest mark from the range should be awarded.
- Where it just meets the standard described, the lowest mark from the range should be awarded.
- Otherwise the mark from the middle of the range should be awarded.

Task

- In pairs, read the following script.
- Use the grid on page 71 to assign a grade.
- As you read through the script, note down three strengths it shows that you might try to emulate in your own writing.
- Finally, read the commentary. Then explain to your partner why the piece has been given its grade.

Reflective writing

Safe beneath the surface

The water undulated around my legs, enveloping me in its gentle embrace. Mesmerised, I glanced down at the shimmering surface of the pool that distortedly mirrored my surroundings. A lone willow was nestled between the translucent beauty of the stars, its cascading leaves swaying in the midnight breeze. I leaned over, but the girl I saw in the water was a stranger. That summer, that night, I was changing before my very eyes.

➡

Wrapping my arms securely around my body, I struggled to remember a time when my mind had been untroubled. I had visited my home in Sicily every summer since the age of two – this was my home, my sanctuary. However, this summer I noticed a change in myself; I was plagued by worries of the year ahead.

The majority of my peers would have no hesitation in saying that secondary one was a frightful year, full of issues with friendships and increasing demands for responsibility. Yet I welcomed the challenge, preferring to keep to myself and focus on my studies. Why was the transition from third to fourth year so difficult?

Battling with my memories, I stole a mouthful of air and pushed off with my arms, quietly slipping beneath the surface. Being underwater had always been my weakness; I revelled in its placidity, never choosing to emerge until my lungs screamed for air.

However, on this night my mind was a turbulent storm, displacing logic and clarity.

My thoughts had turned my sanctuary into a cruel reminder of my childhood – long hours spent without a care in the world. At age five the pool had seemed limitless; as deep as the ocean and as vast as my imagination. Now it seemed pitifully small and shallow.

You see, dear reader, I have an inability to accept change; always have and always will.

Source: SQA Intermediate Writing Folio 2011

Expert commentary

The title is clever and well chosen; it stands for the writer hiding under water and it also shows that she is somewhat reluctant to accept that she has to leave childhood behind and face up to her adult responsibilities.

The first paragraph of the essay has several examples of **effective description** and fairly **deep thinking**. The opening paragraph **sets the scene**: the writer is in a swimming pool in the family's holiday home in Sicily. 'A lone willow was nestled between the translucent beauty of the stars' and we are told that 'the girl I saw in the water was a stranger'. This idea of changing into someone new shows the writer trying to come to terms with growing up and accepting adult responsibilities. The **word choices** are excellent and are used **highly creatively** to bring the descriptions to life for the reader:

undulated … enveloping … embrace … mesmerised … shimmering … distortedly …

Paragraphs 2 and 3 **explore** different stages in the writer's life. In paragraph 2 the **sentencing** is very controlled: 'Wrapping my arms securely around my body, I struggled to remember a time when my mind had been untroubled', and in paragraph 3 the **punctuation** is deployed very well with the effective use of the comma, hyphen, full stop and semi-colon. This, too, could be seen to be an example of the effective and **creative** use of punctuation to highlight meaning.

Paragraphs 4 and 5 are short accounts of her conflicting feelings – being under water has always made her feel carefree but on this occasion her mind is 'a turbulent storm, displacing logic and clarity'. This sentence also shows the use of **effective sentence structure** and again **complex vocabulary**: 'turbulent storm, displacing logic and clarity.'

The final two paragraphs in this extract go on to explain her feelings in more depth. She reflects on the innocence and carefree days of her childhood. The idea of the swimming pool being her sanctuary from responsibility and providing her with positive hope for the future is cleverly reduced in importance through her truthful description, 'Now it seemed pitifully small and shallow.' There is a direct appeal to the reader, 'You see, dear reader', when she sums up her dilemma: 'I have an inability to accept change'. The writing here is mature, shows strong reflection and the writer's personality is clear and convincing. This is very likely to continue as a very good piece of writing.

Hint!

It would be useful here to refer to the grade descriptors on pages 70–71 as you read through the outline of the grade below.

This essay matches the criteria for the highest grade in every respect and it is awarded **15/15** marks.

Technical accuracy

- Meaning is clear at first reading.
- Paragraphing and punctuation are accurate and effective.
- Sentence construction is varied and well controlled.
- Spelling is accurate.

According to the grade descriptors

- Attention to purpose/audience is consistent.
- The piece displays very good creativity, for example with the use of the pool both literally and metaphorically.
- Feelings/reactions/experiences are explored (and we do get the impression that the writer is turning over her feelings in her mind and thinking through them) with a very good degree of self-awareness, insight and sensitivity.
- The features of the chosen genre are deployed effectively, for example in the density of the descriptions.
- Word choice is varied.
- Structure enhances the purpose of the writing.

In fact, it could easily be argued that the quality of this piece of writing **exceeds** the requirements of the 15–13 range.

Task

- In pairs, read the next script.
- Use the grid on page 70 to assign a grade.
- As you read through it, note down three strengths you might try to emulate in your own writing.
- Finally, read the commentary. Then explain to your partner why the piece has been given its grade.

Discursive writing

Phones for you?

Have you ever looked down and witnessed something truly horrifying. Something so horrifying that it makes your hair stand on end and your toes curl. Well I have. I had just finished doing up my fly when I looked down – to my horror – I saw my iphone bobbing in its watery grave. Mobile phones are a central part to everybody's life how will I cope without mine Mobile phones are selling rapidly. Since 1994 a whopping ten billion mobile phones have been sold worldwide, which is more mobile phones than human beings, with five billion mobile phone connections currently in use. Thirty million mobiles are sold in the UK each year alone. But is this widespread use of mobile phones beneficial to society or are they simply another way to waste time?

Mobiles provide simple, quick and cheap communication between family, friends and work. Today a text is only 5p and a call is a mere 10p per minute. Now when a mum needs to tell her kids to come home for dinner she simply needs to phone her child's mobile. Mobile phones are also useful in emergencies. For example if you are involved in an accident with no payphone around all you need to do is to make a call from your mobile. Mobiles are now equipped with 3G internet which allows the user to access the internet on the go. This can be used to send emails. The GPS function built into some mobile phones allows trackers to find people who are lost in the woods or up the mountains. So mobile phones can be the difference between life and death.

Although communication between mobiles is brilliant there is a downside to it. The majority of the working population now have no escape from work. They are in constant contact with their work via email or text or even video call. This can impinge in family life. For example: a family are out at dinner and a parent is emailed on their phone by work. They feel obliged to send an email back. This can be a contributing factor in the separation of many families. Also texting and phoning from a mobile is only cheap when used in moderation. Parents have no control over how many texts their child sends or how many times they update their status on facebook. In 2010 there were 129 billion texts sent worldwide up from 7 billion in 2000. The number of texts being set each year is increasing at an alarming rate. In a report by the Guardian it found that 9 in 10 children under the age of 16 have a mobile phone. So can kids really be trusted not to use their £10 top up in less than a week?

→

Mobiles are becoming increasingly sophisticated. Today we can read a newspaper, watch our favourite film, carry your entire music collection, take photos and videos in HD quality, enjoy a book, catch up on current affairs, play games and if you are old fashioned you might even listen to the radio all on your mobile. A large part of this amazing technology is through applications more commonly known as apps. The apple app store has sold 25 billion paid and free apps since its launch in July 2008. According to apple 'there's an app for just about anything'. Today apps can allow you to check where you parked the car, find a taxi, figure out your share of the bill for a group of friends, read an MRI scan, name a song that is playing on the radio, write a text with your voice, board an aeroplane and even translate languages. Mobile technology just continues to amaze us and I'm ready to see how far it can go.

Source: SQA Intermediate 2 Writing Folio 2012

Expert commentary

In paragraph 1 the writer begins strongly by involving the reader through the use of the **second person**: 'Have **you** ever looked down and witnessed something truly horrifying'. **Humour** is also used to get the reader on side, 'your toes curl', as well as through **parenthesis**, 'to my horror', and the **sentence construction** is nicely balanced, 'Well, I have.' Balanced against these strengths, we also note minor errors, 'to' versus 'of' ('part to everybody's') and a sentencing error, 'how will I cope without mine', as well as the omission of the question mark at the end of the sentence. Following the **engaging description** of his loss, the writer expands the scope of the writing to show the scale of mobile phone sales, 'more mobiles than human beings', and the paragraph ends with the use of the **rhetorical question**, 'or are they another waste of time?'

Paragraph 2 outlines the advantages of mobiles: their speed and affordability, safety and use in emergencies. Throughout the paragraph, there is the impression of a convincing, effective and economical **argument** being presented.

Paragraph 3 examines the disadvantages. Despite the wrong subject–verb agreement, 'the majority … have', the **ideas are used** to **convey a clear line of thought** being pursued at the time. The **vocabulary** is also **varied** and **apt**, for example in **word choices**, such as 'impinge … moderation … alarming'. The pace is hurried and the reader is carried along with a breathless enthusiasm as the arguments are presented.

Paragraph 4 reverts to more advantages. Phones' sophistication is noted and the multiple functions of mobiles used to convince us of their value: newspapers, films, music, photography and videos. The tongue-in-cheek **stance** adopted is also helpful in persuading us to **the point of view** of the writer and so, 'if you are old fashioned you might even listen to the radio all on your mobile.' Again the writer employs the interesting technique of providing us with example after example to support his view and this is a real strength in the piece.

Hint!

It would be useful here to refer to the grade descriptors on pages 70–71 as you read through the outline of the grade below.

Looking at the grade descriptors, we find ourselves in the highest category as the ideas and techniques deployed have a very good degree of objectivity, depth and insight. Attention to purpose is consistent as we can see through the use of a wide range of ideas to support the line of thought. The piece is also very effectively structured to consider both the advantages and disadvantages of mobile phones. The vocabulary is varied, apt and economical and is used to engage the reader. There are errors in the work, but they are few and meaning is still clear at first reading. This is a very good piece of work. It is also substantial.

N.B. It should be noted, though, that this piece of writing goes on to exceed the 1000-word limit. As such, it might be referred to the Principal Assessor and may have a penalty applied. **15/15.**

Technical accuracy

- There are errors in the work, but they are few and meaning is still clear at first reading.
- Paragraphing is accurate and effective.
- Sentence construction is varied and well controlled.
- Spelling is accurate.

According to the grade descriptors

- Attention to purpose is consistent.
- Ideas/techniques deployed have sustained persuasive force and are used to convey a clear line of thought.
- The features of the chosen genre are deployed effectively, for example in the use of humour and rhetorical questions, and in the use of sentence structures of varying lengths.
- Word choice is varied.
- Structure supports the purpose of the writing.

Task

- In pairs, read the following script.
- Use the grid on page 71 to assign a grade.
- As you read through it, note down three strengths you might try to emulate in your own writing.
- Finally, read the commentary. Then explain to your partner why the piece has been given its grade.

Personal writing

Has the game changed?

Has there been any change in the world of rugby? I would say so, but not for the good. The main speculation of changes in today's game is the Scrum, lack of consistency in referees and the countless kicking which throws away good game momentum. The head of rugby, the IRB need to bring in knew laws to bring back the twentieth century style of play.

➜

In this days game it take an average of four minutes for a scrum to be completed. This has ruined the game to watch because of its stop start pattern through out the eighty minutes. This has been complained about over half a million times in the last year, and the IRB (International Rugby Board) have failed to address this severe problem in the game. The scrum has always had a lot of criticism, the main reason being the amount of strain going down each player's necks, and when a scrum collapses it can cause severe damage and can cause permanent paralysis or even death. Most of the criticism about scrums come from worried parents that there child is in danger of serious injury, to be honest, if these parents are going to moan and complain, then don't let there child play, simple. The scrum doesn't really affect my game because I play with the backs, but it is very frustrating when scrums collapse every five minutes and the referee fails to address the perpetrator. On average there is a ton of weight going down each professional player's neck; you can even hear the crunch between the opposing team's necks after the referee commands the engage. The scrum has changed dramatically in the last twenty years, they used to actually charge at each other and stamp on one another with there studs, which was deemed to be normal, well at least until someone lost an eye. These problems must be addressed to open up the game and create fast running rugby, like the southern hemisphere teams, a good example of this is the famous All Blacks, Notable for there high tempo game which is almost impossible to close down.

Source: SQA Intermediate 2 Understanding Standards 2011

Expert commentary

This piece of writing crosses two forms – personal experience and discursive – but perhaps works best for the writer if it is judged as a **personal experience**.

The writer deals with a significant experience in his life, how he feels about changes to a game he cares about – rugby – in paragraph 1.

This sense of significance comes across in paragraph 2 as the writer uses **word choices** to convey emotion: 'ruined … complained … failed.' Some sentences are well controlled: 'The scrum doesn't really affect my game because I play with the backs, but it is very frustrating when scrums collapse every five minutes and the referee fails to address the perpetrator.' Others are not, and these are in the majority. Very often, **punctuation** is inaccurate. The expression, 'a good example of this,' for instance, should begin with a **capital letter**.

Although the **meaning is clear**, and **feelings come across with a sense of involvement**, the **expression** here could be described as **adequate** on balance, although there are times when it is **clumsy**, for example 'The main speculation of changes in today's game is the Scrum, lack of consistency in referees and the countless kicking which throws away good game momentum.' Sometimes the wrong words are chosen, 'knew' in the first paragraph being a good example, and words are also confused, for example 'there' instead of 'their'. **Apostrophes** are also omitted: 'In this days game.'

Hint!

It would be useful here to refer to the grade descriptors on pages 70–71 as you read through the outline of the grade below.

This essay is a **reasonably well-sustained** piece of writing, with a **sense of involvement**. It just achieves the standard required for a pass, and has been given **8/15**.

Technical accuracy

- There are some lapses in paragraphing. The second paragraph, for example, is quite lengthy.
- Sentencing and punctuation have a number of inaccuracies, but the spelling is mostly accurate. There are some formal errors, although these are not deemed enough to fail the piece.

According to the grade descriptors

- Attention to purpose and audience is reasonably well sustained.
- Feelings/reactions/experiences are explored with a sense of involvement.
- The features of the chosen genre are deployed with a degree of success, for example in the use of emotionally charged language in, 'dramatically ... severe ... frustrating.'
- Word choice is effective, in the main.
- A discernible structure is evident, which is appropriate to purpose.

This gives you a good idea of a baseline pass – the minimum standard acceptable for a pass.

Task

- In pairs, read the script below.
- Use the grid on page 70 to assign a grade.
- As you read through it, note down three strengths you might try to emulate in your own writing.
- Finally, read the commentary. Then explain to your partner why the piece has been given its grade.

Discursive Essay

Problems Faced by Teenagers in Today's Society

1 There are many problems facing teenagers in society today. The main problems facing teenagers today are Parents, Money, Media, Teachers, School and Rules/Laws.

2 The problems that occur between Parents and Teenagers are that on the one hand Parents are always telling you to grow up and act your age as well as at the same time they treat you like a child. The Parental outlook to this is that after they look after you, protect you, clothe you, feed you and put a roof over your head.

3 The problems that are always ongoing for teenagers in today's society with regards to money are that they need money to cover things like Birthdays, Easter, Christmas and so on. However to do this they need to get a part time job after school or at the week end but due to their age they cannot get a job or they have too much homework after school, so they cannot work after school.

4 Teenagers are given a raw deal when it comes to the media, because every time that they portray a teenager in the television or on the radio they always show them smoking, drinking, fighting or taking drugs. Although some teenagers actually do these things that the media portrays not every teenager does so therefore it is not right to put all teenagers as one in the same.

→

5   Some people say that the violent video games that teenagers play can actually turn them violent.

6   Teenagers have problems with their Teachers because they think that they are given too much study material for their upcoming exams, or they have supported learning classes at lunchtime or after school. They also feel that the Teachers push them too hard and apply a lot of pressure on them to pass their exams.

7   Teenagers have problems with school because they think that the teachers are too strict, when in fact what the teachers are actually doing are preparing us for the outside world after school, like getting a good job, they do this by sending us on work experience for a week to give us an insight into what awaits us on the outside world when we leave school. Teenagers also feel that school hours are very long and tiring, you get very little time to rest and relax during term time. One plus about School for Teenagers is that you get lots of breaks and holidays.

8   There are many Rules/Laws for Teenagers nowadays, some are very practical whereas some are very stupid and unnecessary. Teenagers think that some of these laws are not fair like only 2 or 3 schoolchildren in a shop at the one time because this to help the shopkeeper keep an eye on the kids and prevent stealing not every teenager is out to steal from them. There are certain rules that Teenagers think are right are rules such as Speed Limits, Selling Alcohol to under 18s, Cigarettes to under 16s are put in place to protect them and for their own benefit.

Source: S Grade Folio 2009

Expert commentary

This script is a transactional piece of writing where the candidate has been asked to give an account of the difficulties faced by young people in today's society. You may wish to consider their treatment by adults, parents, teachers and the police.

This piece shares elements of both conveying information and discursive writing. The opening paragraph lists the main problems facing teenagers, drawn from the title, and then goes on to deal with each of these in turn.

In paragraph 2, the problem with parents is that they, 'are always telling you to grow up and act your age', following which the candidate attempts to view the problem from a parental perspective, 'The parental outlook to this is ...'

Paragraph 3 states that teenagers 'need money to cover things like birthdays, Easter ...' and the dilemma of teenagers being unable to earn money, 'due to their age' is cited.

The portrayal of teenagers in the media is dealt with in a little more detail in paragraph 4 and we have another attempt to consider an alternative point of view and so, 'although some teenagers actually do these things ... not every teenager does ... therefore it is not right.'

Paragraph 5 only offers the opinion regarding the pressure placed on teenagers by teachers, but paragraph 6 is more substantial, dealing with 'problems with school'. In this paragraph, the writer shifts towards a more discursive approach in looking at the advantages and disadvantages of the school experience for teenagers.

The piece ends with a final paragraph (8) dealing with 'rules/laws'. Here, the writer tries to offer a balanced view about rules for teenagers by saying that, 'some are very practical whereas some are very stupid and unnecessary' and the piece concludes with the writer stating that teenagers do recognise that certain rules, 'are put in place to protect them'.

In terms of technical accuracy, sentence construction and punctuation have a number of inaccuracies, 'the parental outlook to this' for example, and the long sentence in paragraph 3, 'However to do this they need to get a part time job after school or at the week end but due to their age they cannot get a job or they have too much homework after school, so they cannot work after school'. There is also inappropriate capitalisation in 'Speed Limits, Selling Alcohol ... Cigarettes'. Some re-reading is necessary, and the ideas presented are not always convincing, offering opinion and assertion without supporting evidence. Meaning is not always clear at first reading. This piece would, therefore, not achieve the minimum standard for technical accuracy.

Turning to the grade descriptors, we find ourselves in the fourth box.

- Attention to purpose and audience is evident but is **not always sustained** with the crossover, for example between conveying information and discursive writing.

- Information selected shows a little evidence of appropriate research, but is not always presented in a manner that enhances meaning.

- The stance tends towards the personal/anecdotal.

- There is an attempt to deploy the features of the chosen genre, by considering alternative viewpoints, for example.

- Word choice lacks variety.

- Structure is not entirely appropriate to purpose, although there is some evidence of structure – the introductory paragraph lists the problems and the writer deals with each of these problems in turn, but the information is not always presented in a manner that enhances meaning.

6/15.

Brings us into the 'fail' category.

CHAPTER SIX

BARRIERS TO SUCCESS: TACKLING COMMON ERRORS

For many years, Principal Assessors have been producing reports on what worked well in students' writing and what didn't. Every year, without fail, they mention the topics covered below. If you study these topics and take them on board, you stand a much better chance of success in your portfolio. Singly, one of them does not necessarily mean you have a problem; collectively, they would represent **significant technical inaccuracies** and may fail you.

Conference calls allow you to 'phone a friend' by giving you **answers and explanations**. This can help you to work out **why** an answer is correct.

Try the following on your own **then see the answers in Chapter 7**.

The comma splice

Conference call 1

One of the most common technical problems facing writers is the comma splice. To 'splice' means to 'join', and the comma splice is used when we join two sentences together (technically, as two independent clauses) using a comma rather than a full stop.

Task

Read these examples and decide if they make sense:

Paul was a humble man. He never got the credit he deserved.

Mary liked to read. She would read anything.

Sharif couldn't sit still. He just wanted to move around all the time.

More comma splicing?

Conference call 2

Task

Now do the same with these:

Julie walked to the store, she chatted to Jacqui on her way there.

Saul was tired, he simply wanted to lie down.

Sarah limped to the first-aid room, she desperately needed help.

Commas

Conference call 3

The use of commas

We use a comma:

Use	Example
to separate things in a list	'Potatoes, spinach, and sprouts are all awful.'
to complete sentences	'While you clean the windows, I will polish the table.'
to join sentences	'Peter was good at English, but he was brilliant at chemistry.'
to create a pause between sentences	'If you finish your coffee, we could go to the zoo.'
to replace brackets	'Our teacher, Mr Mitchell, is a great man.'
to introduce quotations	'Will asked, "Are you coming to dinner?"'
after an introduction	'Well, that would appear to be that!'

Task

Try these:

1. Having tired myself out at school all day I like swimming in my local pool.
2. Horse-riding requires patience agility and determination.
3. Anna a friend of John's wanted to come to visit in the New Year.
4. He was clever but he was not always subtle.
5. So you need to consider the needs of your audience.

The punctuation of direct speech

Conference call 4

Speech marks ("   " or '   ') are used to show the words actually spoken by someone during a conversation, as it is very important that we know **who** is saying **what** to **whom**. This punctuation is used also to separate the **speaker** from the words **spoken**.

The rules

1. We show that two different people are speaking by putting what they say on separate lines:

'Did you see my new iPhone?'   asked Peter.

| Words spoken | | Speaker |

'Yes. It's terrific,'   replied Jill.

| Words spoken | | Speaker |

2. The actual words spoken should be enclosed in inverted commas, "   " or '   ':

'Yes,' replied Jill. 'It's terrific.'

3. There should be a comma, full stop, question mark or exclamation mark at the end of a piece of speech. This is placed inside the inverted comma or commas:

'You might win,' he said.

> Comma

John said, 'I don't expect to win.'

> Full stop

'Can I play, too?' he asked.

> Question mark

'No!' she shouted.

> Exclamation mark

4. If direct speech comes after the information about who is speaking, you should use a comma to introduce the piece of speech, placed before the first inverted comma:

Bill said, 'This is easy.'

5. If the direct speech is broken up by information about who is speaking, you need a comma (or a question mark or exclamation mark) to end the first piece of speech **and** a full stop or another comma before the second piece (before the inverted comma or commas):

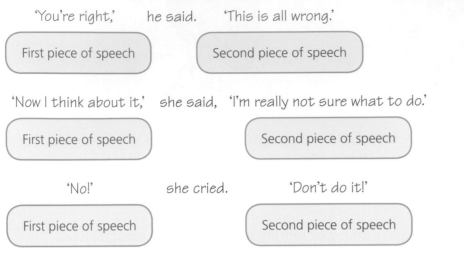

'You're right,'   he said.   'This is all wrong.'

| First piece of speech | | Second piece of speech |

'Now I think about it,'   she said,   'I'm really not sure what to do.'

| First piece of speech | | Second piece of speech |

'No!'   she cried.   'Don't do it!'

| First piece of speech | | Second piece of speech |

Changing word order

I gave you an order!

Changing the order of words varies your sentences, makes them more interesting, and maintains the readers' attention.

Often the word order looks like this:

'Leave me out of it,'   said   Sheila.

| Word(s) spoken | Speaker |

Sometimes this order can be reversed:

Joe   said,   'I want to leave now.'

| Speaker | Word(s) spoken |

And sometimes the order looks like this.

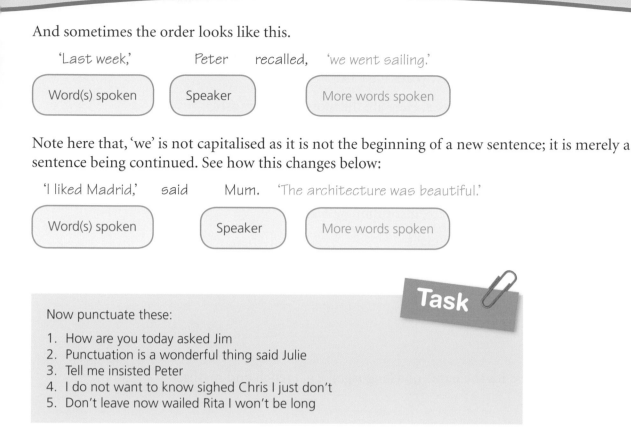

'Last week,' Peter recalled, 'we went sailing.'

| Word(s) spoken | Speaker | More words spoken |

Note here that, 'we' is not capitalised as it is not the beginning of a new sentence; it is merely a sentence being continued. See how this changes below:

'I liked Madrid,' said Mum. 'The architecture was beautiful.'

| Word(s) spoken | Speaker | More words spoken |

Task

Now punctuate these:

1. How are you today asked Jim
2. Punctuation is a wonderful thing said Julie
3. Tell me insisted Peter
4. I do not want to know sighed Chris I just don't
5. Don't leave now wailed Rita I won't be long

Sentencing

This is another area where students face difficulties. This can be because of poor **punctuation** (using commas rather than full stops), which we covered earlier, poor **capitalisation** (failing to begin a sentence with a capital letter), or because the **expression** is poor, making the meaning unclear. This can be as a result of confused **tenses**, weak **grammar** (such as wrong **subject–verb agreement**) or even poor **spelling**. We shall now address these key concerns.

Capitalisation

We have seen this as a problem even in some of the samples used in this book, and it has been cited as a growing problem over the last few years. Take heed!

Capitals are used in a great many cases. Here are the most common uses:

- to start a sentence or a fragment, e.g. 'Tired!'
- to name days of the week and months of the year
- to name languages or nationalities
- for proper names, of a person, place, institution or event
- for titles of things, e.g. books and plays
- to show the pronoun 'I'.

Don't use them for:

- emphasis
- seasons
- school subjects (unless it's the name of a language), e.g. French and maths.

Confused tenses

Over the years, SQA markers have noted that students often confuse their tenses. Broadly, tenses should be **consistent**; that is, if a story is set in the past, then it should continue in the past. You may wish to mix tenses if you are using a flashback technique, for example, but this should be a deliberate undertaking on your part.

Very often, the **simple past tense** ('he went to the shops' – but is no longer doing it now) is confused with the **present perfect tense** ('he has gone to the shops' – and may still be doing it – or not!).

This confusion is often expressed in formulations such as 'The bell has went.'

> ## Hint!
> The simple past doesn't need an auxiliary verb ('has' or 'have') to do its job, but the present perfect tense does need this help.

Pluperfect tense (sometimes called past perfect)

This tense is formed by the use of the auxiliary verb **'had'** + **the past participle**:

Had

Auxiliary verb

learned.

Past participle

Had

Auxiliary verb

taught.

Past participle

This tense shows an action completed before a specified or implied past time, in other words an action before another action, both of which happened in the past:

When I arrived,

At some time in the past.

Sally had gone.

Before I arrived.

Note that this is entirely different from the simple past:

When I arrived,

At some time in the past.

Sally went.

Not before, but **as** I arrived.

Subject–verb agreement

Conference call 5

This is a very common problem for students.

Let's try a little assessment!

Identify the correct word and then check your answers in Chapter 7, where the answers are explained.

1. Twenty pounds **is/are** a lot of money.
2. One of my friends **has/have** spoken to my teacher.
3. There **is/are** a range of options.
4. A vase of flowers and a bowl **sit/sits** on the table.
5. A pair of sunglasses **is/are** £10.
6. The team **is/are** playing next week.
7. Some of you **is/are** eager to get home.
8. Bill and his friends **has/have** decided to join the team.
9. There **is/are** apples, oranges and pears available.
10. Few students **enjoy/enjoys** exam preparation classes after school.

Common confusions

Conference call 6

- Where/were
  - **Where** means **in which place**.
  - **Were** means **have been**.
- Their/there
  - **Their** means **belonging to them**.
  - **There** means **in that place**.
- Gone/went
  - **Gone** needs help from **have**, **has**, **had**, **is** or **are**.
  - **Went** does not. It stands on its own.
- Saw/seen
  - **Seen** needs help from **have**, **has**, **had**, **is** or **are**.
  - **Saw** does not. It stands on its own.
- I and me
  - I **carries out** an action.
  - Me **receives** an action.

Task

Identify the correct word and then check your answers!

1. This is the place **where/were** I first met him.
2. **Where/were** you late for school this morning?
3. Last month we **where/were** in Australia.
4. I've **never** been **there/their** before.
5. It's **there/their** secret.
6. The money is over **there/their**.
7. He **has went/went** too far with that joke.
8. All the money **has gone/has went**.
9. I **seen/saw** it coming.
10. I **seen/saw** the light!
11. **Me/I** and my friends Rick, Pete and Jane went shopping.
12. She sat next to Tim and **I/me**.

Apostrophes

Conference call 7

These are used in two cases:

1. To show belonging:

Willie's iPod.

> Shows that the iPod belongs to Willie.

The viewers' choice.

> Here, we are referring to more than one viewer.

James' essay **or** James's essay.

> Shows the essay belongs to James.

2. To show a missing letter(s):

It's just too late.

> Shows that that the letter **i** has been missed out. 'It's' here is short for 'it is'.

He'll be there. Don't worry!

> Here, two letters are missed out. The **wi** of the word 'will'.

Task

Are these apostrophes correct or incorrect?

1. The dog wagged **it's** tail.
2. **Its** been a long, tiring day.
3. **Yesterday's** weather was terrible.
4. Kindness brings **it's** own rewards.
5. I took 300 **euro's** on holiday.
6. We had **panini's** for lunch.
7. **Roger's** record still stands today.
8. I remember the **1990's** well.
9. **Bobs'** birthday is on Monday.
10. **Its** simply too complicated to explain.
11. The **children's** hearing was yesterday.
12. The **womens'** group met today.

Word order

Conference call 8

Varying the order of words in your sentences can make a huge difference. It can make your writing far more interesting.

In the above example, we find out about the stranger. Then we learn **what** he is doing (stood) after which we discover **how** he is doing this (quietly) and **where** (outside).

This word order puts the stranger at the centre of things. Consider how things change in the next example:

The **theme** of the sentence has now changed and the idea of menace has been heightened – just by changing the order of words.

Task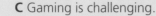

How might you alter the word order in the sentences below? Now describe the effects of the changes.

1. Something wicked walks this way.
2. He took up his belongings and ran quickly.
3. We are strong together.
4. The car stopped suddenly.
5. We walked unsteadily.

Topic sentences

Conference call 9

Paragraphing

Often, in students' writing, paragraphs are simply absent, but they are vital to the organisation of your writing. They show order, thought and structure. They allow you to select and highlight what is most significant in your writing. They also help the reader to follow what you are trying to communicate by breaking the text up into manageable bits.

What are they?

Paragraphs are groups of sentences joined together by a similar idea or topic.

How are they structured?

Key sentences, sometimes called **topic sentences**, are often found at the beginning of paragraphs.

How do we recognise them?

New paragraphs start on a **new line** and are often **indented** from the margin.

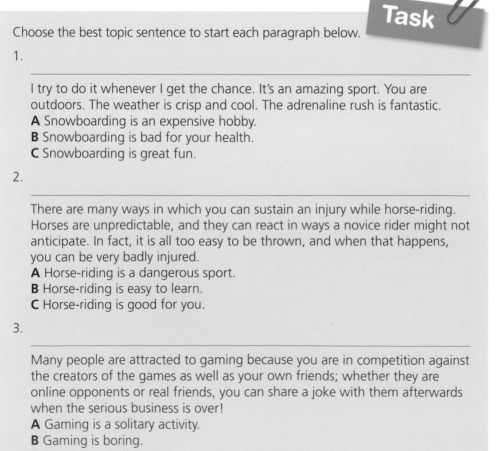

Task

Choose the best topic sentence to start each paragraph below.

1.

_____

I try to do it whenever I get the chance. It's an amazing sport. You are outdoors. The weather is crisp and cool. The adrenaline rush is fantastic.
A Snowboarding is an expensive hobby.
B Snowboarding is bad for your health.
C Snowboarding is great fun.

2.

_____

There are many ways in which you can sustain an injury while horse-riding. Horses are unpredictable, and they can react in ways a novice rider might not anticipate. In fact, it is all too easy to be thrown, and when that happens, you can be very badly injured.
A Horse-riding is a dangerous sport.
B Horse-riding is easy to learn.
C Horse-riding is good for you.

3.

_____

Many people are attracted to gaming because you are in competition against the creators of the games as well as your own friends; whether they are online opponents or real friends, you can share a joke with them afterwards when the serious business is over!
A Gaming is a solitary activity.
B Gaming is boring.
C Gaming is challenging.

Supporting sentences

Conference call 10

A supporting sentence develops the main idea in the topic sentence. It adds details to the topic.

Task

Identify the supporting sentences in these paragraphs.
Are any of the sentences irrelevant?

1   There is a range of reasons why I despise physics. I can't do it for a start. It makes no sense to me. I just can't seem to grasp the concepts. I hate it!
2   Internet use is growing exponentially. In the early 1980s very few computers were connected to the Internet. By the year 2000, there were over 70 million. Internet use also seems to be gaining a foothold in many different countries; not just the developed West. I don't use it much, though.
3   Going to the gym has many health benefits. It has been proven medically that cardiovascular training is very good for your heart and lungs and helps to prevent heart disease and strokes. There is a variety of machines to help you work out. It is also very good for you in terms of boosting your strength. Weight training, for example, not only builds strength, it also tones the muscles.

How are they joined or signposted?

Surprises can be a good thing, but often what comes in the next paragraph will be suggested by the previous paragraph. **Linking words and phrases**, too, can be helpful in creating a **flow** between paragraphs. These words/phrases can be grouped according to the jobs they do.

Sequence	firstly
	next
	in addition
	in conclusion
	to summarise
	further
	another
Addition	and
	in addition (to)
	furthermore
	also
	too
	as well as

Contrast	however
	nevertheless
	nonetheless
	still
	although
	though
	but
	yet
	in contrast
	on the contrary
Result	so
	as a result
	as a consequence
	therefore
	thus
	hence
	due to
	as such
Reason	for
	because
	since
	as
	because of
Comparison	similarly
	also
	like
	just as
	similar to
	compared with
Emphasis	indeed
	undoubtedly
	obviously
	generally
	admittedly
	especially
	importantly
Example	for example
	for instance
	such as
	including
	namely

Linking words and phrases

Conference call 11

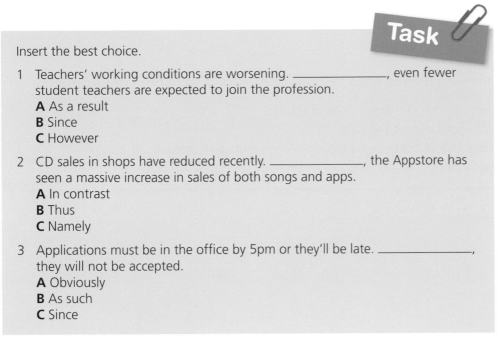

Task

Insert the best choice.

1 Teachers' working conditions are worsening. _____, even fewer student teachers are expected to join the profession.
   A As a result
   B Since
   C However

2 CD sales in shops have reduced recently. _____, the Appstore has seen a massive increase in sales of both songs and apps.
   A In contrast
   B Thus
   C Namely

3 Applications must be in the office by 5pm or they'll be late. _____, they will not be accepted.
   A Obviously
   B As such
   C Since

Sense and nonsense

The following sentences formed the description of a recent TV programme. Can you spot the problem?

Peter Manuel committed several murders in Scotland in the 1950s for which he was hanged. He later admitted to many more murders.

Spot the error

Conference call 12

Task

What is wrong with these sentences?

1 The firm are proud to have served our clients for 30 years.
2 Pete and Jane's applications were both late.
3 The nurse advised the sick girl to lay on the bed.
4 Jill was now quite a bit pregnant.
5 Jo found herself in a very unique situation.

Finally!

It is easier than you think to write something less than perfect. Don't be caught out! **Re-read what you have written and make changes when necessary.**

Apps

You might find the following **iPhone apps** helpful. They are available from the App Store:

- **ACGrammar1** covers common grammatical issues.
- **Spelling1** deals with confused spellings.
- **TrickyWords1** shows the difference between words that are often confused.
- **Punctuate** deals with punctuation rules.

Best of luck with your portfolio.

CHAPTER SEVEN

ANSWERS TO CONFERENCE CALLS

Conference call 1

It makes perfect sense. There are two sentences and they are separated by a full stop. They could, however, be joined through the use of the conjunction 'but' to make a more logically linked single sentence:

Paul was a humble man, but he never got the credit he deserved.

The two sentences making up example 2, however, could be linked more coherently through the use of an adverb such as, 'Indeed' or 'In fact':

Mary liked to read. She would read anything.

In the final example, a logical connective such as 'because' could replace the full stop:

Sharif couldn't sit still. He just wanted to move around all the time.

Conference call 2

You might be tempted to say this makes sense; it doesn't. This is an example of the comma splice. The first part, 'Julie walked to the store …', is a sentence in its own right. It makes sense in its own right. We don't need to know that she chatted to her friend Jacqui on the way. That's another sentence again, about another topic, and starts with the new subject pronoun: '**She** chatted to Jacqui on her way there.' This might make us think about who 'she' is, if it were on its own, and we might also wonder about where 'there' is precisely, but it would still make sense, so it is a sentence in its own right.

This is the same in example 2. 'Saul was tired' is a sentence. It makes sense in its own right. We might want to know why he was tired, but that would be the subject of another sentence. To correct this, we'd need to remove the comma and add a full stop: 'He simply wanted to lie down.'

The third example is very similar. We might be tempted to use a comma as the part after the comma explains why Sarah has gone to the medical room, but this would be wrong. It begins a new subject and, as such, the subject changes (slightly) from 'Sarah' to 'she'.

Sarah limped to the first aid room. She desperately needed help. ✓

Sarah limped to the first aid room, she desperately needed help. ✗

Conference call 3

1. 'Having tired myself out at school all day, I like swimming in my local pool.'
2. 'Horse-riding requires patience, agility, and determination', **or** 'Horse riding requires patience, agility and determination.' In modern usage, the serial comma used before the co-ordinating conjunction 'and' is becoming less common.
3. 'Anna, a friend of John's, wanted to come to visit in the New Year.'
4. 'He was clever, but he was not always subtle', **or** 'He was clever but he was not always subtle.' In modern usage, the serial comma used before the co-ordinating conjunction 'but' is becoming less common.
5. 'So, you need to consider the needs of your audience.'

Conference call 4

1. 'How are you today?' asked Jim.
2. 'Punctuation is a wonderful thing,' said Julie.
3. 'Tell me!' insisted Peter.
4. 'I do not want to know,' sighed Chris. 'I just don't.'
5. 'Don't leave now,' wailed Rita. 'I won't be long.'

Conference call 5

1. 'Twenty pounds is a lot of money.' An amount of money is a singular, but the pounds themselves are plural, e.g. 'Pounds **are** often used in foreign countries instead of the local currency.'
2. 'One of my friends has spoken to my teacher.' Singular subject: one.
3. 'There is a range of options.' One range, singular again. 'Options' is not the subject. This catches out many people!
4. 'A vase of flowers and a bowl sit on the table.' Two subjects make a plural so use the plural form of the verb.
5. 'A pair of sunglasses is £10.' Refers to one pair so this is singular.
6. 'The team is playing next week.' This sounds odd, but collective nouns like 'team' take the singular.
7. 'Some of you are eager to get home.' 'Some' could be singular or plural, but here it is plural as it refers to more than one member of a larger group.
8. 'Bill and his friends have decided to join the team.' Here, there are two subjects: one singular (Bill) and one plural (friends). The verb agrees with the subject closest to it in these cases; in this case 'friends', which is a plural.
9. 'There are apples, oranges and pears available.' Use the plural form of the verb when the subjects are joined by 'and'.
10. 'Few students enjoy exam preparation classes after school.' The indefinite pronouns 'few', 'both', 'many', 'several' are always plural.

Conference call 6

1. 'This is the place where I first met him.'
2. 'Were you late for school this morning?'
3. 'Last month we were in Australia.'
4. 'I've never been there before.'
5. 'It's their secret.'
6. 'The money is over there.'
7. 'He went too far with that joke.'
8. 'All the money has gone.'
9. 'I saw it coming.'
10. 'I saw the light!'
11. 'I and my friends Rick, Pete and Jane went shopping.'
12. 'She sat next to Tim and me.'

Conference call 7

1. Incorrect. The apostrophe here would stand for **it is**. 'The dog wagged it is tail' is not what the writer is trying to communicate.
2. Incorrect. Here **It's** would mean **It has**, which would make sense here.
3. Correct. The weather belonging to yesterday.
4. Incorrect. No apostrophe required. No letters are missing and there is no shortening.
5. Incorrect. **Euros** is simply the plural of **euro**.
6. Incorrect. **Panini** is already a plural (the singular is **panino**). Equally, there are no letters missing and there is no shortening.
7. Correct.
8. Incorrect. There are no letters missing and there is no shortening.
9. Incorrect. The apostrophe should be between 'b' and 's', i.e. **Bob's**.
10. Incorrect. An apostrophe is required: **It's**, short for **It is**.
11. Correct.
12. Incorrect. Women is already a plural. It should be written **women's**.

Conference call 8

1. 'Something wicked this way walks.' This slows down the pace of the sentence, makes it more menacing and creates the impression of footsteps treading towards us!
2. 'Quickly, he took up his belongings and ran.' Here, we have the idea of haste both at the beginning and at the end of the sentence, so the idea of speed is emphasised.
3. 'Together, we are strong.' The ideas of togetherness and strength are both emphasised by this word order.
4. 'Suddenly, the car stopped.' The idea of a rapid halt is emphasised by placing the word 'suddenly' at the start of the sentence.
5. 'Unsteadily, we walked.' The emphasis is changed from the act of walking to how the walking was done – unsteadily.

Conference call 9

1. **C** The paragraph is full of positive references to snowboarding and how much the speaker enjoys taking part in it. The other options may be true, but they are not mentioned in the paragraph and, therefore, could not form a topic sentence for this paragraph.

2. **A** Everything in the paragraph relates to the danger presented by horse-riding. It may also be easy to learn and it may also be good for you, but we don't know that from the information given in this paragraph.

3. **C** The paragraph does not make it seem as if gaming is either solitary or boring. The idea of competition, however, is mentioned, and from this we can gather that the topic sentence should be about challenge.

Conference call 10

1. 'There is a range of reasons why I despise physics.' is a topic sentence.

   'I can't do it for a start. It makes no sense to me. I just can't seem to grasp the concepts.' are all supporting sentences.

   'I hate it!' is not a supporting statement. It is not one of the reasons why the speaker despises physics; it is a repeat of the fact that the speaker dislikes the subject intensely.

2. 'Internet use is growing exponentially.' is a topic sentence.

   'In the early 1980s very few computers were connected to the Internet. By the year 2000 there were over 70 million. Internet use also seems to be gaining a foothold in many different countries; not just the developed West.' are all supporting sentences.

   'I don't use it much, though.' is irrelevant, as it does not give an example of the growth in the use of the Internet, which is the subject of this paragraph.

3. 'Going to the gym has many health benefits.' is a topic sentence.

   'It has been proven medically that cardiovascular training is very good for your heart and lungs and helps to prevent heart disease and strokes. It is also very good for you in terms of boosting your strength. Weight training, for example, not only builds strength – it also tones the muscles.' are all supporting sentences, as they continue the idea of the benefits of going to the gym.

   'There is a variety of machines to help you work out.' is an irrelevant sentence as it does not add any information about the health benefits of going to the gym.

Conference call 11

1. **A** is the best option. It shows the result of the worsening conditions. The use of B would suggest that teachers' conditions are worsening because of the fact that fewer student teachers are expected to join the profession. Option C would suggest that there is a contrast going on – which there isn't.

2. **A** is the best option. It shows the contrast between CD sales in shops and the sales of both songs and apps in the Appstore. B would suggest that the Appstore's increasing sales are as a result of the drop in sales of CDs in shops. C just doesn't make sense.

3. **B** is the best option. It shows the result or the consequences of lateness. A is not entirely appropriate as it is not obvious that late applications won't be accepted, although this is likely. C does not make sense.

Conference call 12

1. 'The firm' is a collective term. It therefore takes a singular verb, 'is'. 'Our' is a first person plural possessive adjective. It is the plural of the singular 'my'. The subject of the sentence is singular and neuter – 'the firm' – so it should take a singular neuter agreement, 'its'.

2. It could be interpreted that Jane is the owner of both applications. What's the easy solution? 'Pete's and Jane's applications were both late.'

3. 'Lay' is the wrong verb to use here. It means to put something down. 'Lie' is the intended verb, which means to assume a resting position.

4. 'Quite' means 'absolutely' or 'completely'. Recently, it has been thought to mean 'a little bit'. This example shows the distinction clearly.

5. 'Unique' means 'the only one of its kind'. There cannot, therefore, be degrees of uniqueness.